ESOTERIC
PATH

GW00469770

The ESOTERIC PATH

An Introduction to the Hermetic Tradition

LUC BENOIST

Translated with an additional chapter by
Robin Waterfield

This Edition First Published 1988
English translation and text © Robin Waterfield 1988
Original © Presses Universitaires de France 1963

All rights reserved. No part of this book may be reproduced or utilized in any form or by any means, electronic or mechanical, including photocopying, recording, or by any information storage and retrieval system, without permission in writing from the Publisher.

British Library Cataloguing in Publication Data

Benoist, Luc
The esoteric path: an introduction to the
Hermetic tradition.
1. Esotericism
I. Title II. L'esoterisme. *English*
135'.4

ISBN 0 85030 645 0

Crucible is an imprint of The Aquarian Press, part of the Thorsons Publishing Group, Wellingborough, Northamptonshire NN8 2RQ, England

Printed in Great Britain by Woolnough Bookbinding Limited,
Irthlingborough, Northamptonshire
Typeset by MJL Limited, Hitchin, Hertfordshire

1 3 5 7 9 10 8 6 4 2

Contents

Introduction

Introduction

The world only survives
because of the secret.
Sepher Ha-Zohar

Readers of a collection as modern as the series *Que Sais-Je?* may perhaps be surprised to find a study on esoteric teachings included in it. The doctrines of esoterism which this work discusses are amongst those which modern science considers as outmoded and archaic and not possessing any precise objective capable of experimental proof. Adopting such a position, however, confuses science and technology with reason. For if it is logical to respect the principles of rationality which are not in doubt, it is not logical to limit their application. 'Every system is true in what it affirms and false in what it denies', said Leibnitz, one of the founders of infinitesimal calculus. Every negation cuts off an element of the possible from reality, an element which it is the task of science to elucidate. So it is illogical to reduce everything to its rational and technological aspects, valuable as these are in their own domains. The ancient history of primitive man is also a part of the domain of science. And is it not obvious that modern man as he lives and functions remains to a great extent primitive, and how much his demands remain archaic and irrational? Simply from the point of view of technology the most perfect machine does not abolish the original tool or the primitive function it claims to replace. The supersonic aeroplane does not abolish the use of our legs. The calculator does not prevent the human brain from reasoning as it pleases. Agricultural chemistry still has to pay attention to the law of the seasons and the progress of the sun. The most ambitious calculation of human needs still has to take account of human sensitivity and spirituality which it can never satisfy. Morals, intuition, religion, contemplation, will always elude a general mechanistic approach.

In return, the universal law of balance demands that in compensation for this general materialism an equivalent freedom be granted to the superior claims of the spirit. Esoterism or the inner way provides the best means of supplying this balance. Firstly its role is to furnish the means of understanding the sacred writings of ancient civilizations, both eastern and western. These writings have until recently seemed to be impenetrably mysterious, although in reality they describe a perennial reality and only their expression of it obscures its topical relevance. Then they enable us to grasp the true nature of our own tradition and the aspirations which it satisfies. So even the most modern of men, provided they have remained near enough to their own inner natures to give due respect to the unknown world within them, will become able to grasp a secret which can be confided to them only by allusion.

In the first part of the book our exposition has used the work of René Guénon as a guide; his language, logical and almost mathematical, used to explain superrational truths, serves as a symbolic means of conveying these truths. His metaphysical point of view serves as an introduction to the second part which is concerned with the inner aspects of the principal world religions and of the inner meaning of the initiatory ceremonies to be found in them.

The point of view which Guénon's work provides for us gained our assent because of its logical and universal character independent of any system, of all dogma, and free of all religious or linguistic bias. However, considerations of length have compelled us to make very compressed summaries and while we have made every effort to avoid superficiality, we do not claim always to have been successful. As a result we have had to ignore all but the major doctrines. Our sole objective, in spite of the lure of many attractive side issues, has been to offer precision and exactitude in a domain from which they are generally noticeably absent.

Some may perhaps regret that we have not given space to the use by certain writers and poets of a certain natural esoterism, arising from symbolism and surrealism, and no less in its use by certain modern adherents of structuralism. The enlightened reader will himself be easily able to make such connections. He will understand that no doctrine invalidates any other doctrine or particular points of view about a reality which is so multiform and so mysterious.

The occasional relative nature of these different points of view does not imply that the inner knowledge which the different forms and structures claim to embrace is also relative, but merely bears witness to the limitations of our means of expression. Esoteric teaching which endeavours to reveal this interior knowledge (without having the means to avoid all imprecision) does permit us to transcend all cultural forms and to attain to those invariable constants in which is hidden the ineffable essence of the truth.

PART ONE

GENERAL CONSIDERATIONS

1.

Exoteric and Esoteric

From a comprehensive viewpoint one finds amongst certain Greek philosophers the notion of esoteric teaching applied to a form of oral instruction given to chosen disciples. Although it is difficult under such circumstances to be sure of the nature of such teaching, one may reasonably deduce from the conditions under which it was given that this teaching went far beyond philosophy and rational exposition to arrive at a quite different level of truth designed to impart wisdom which would penetrate the entire being of the pupil both mind and spirit. Such would seem to have been true of the teachings of Pythagoras which via Plato were transmitted to the neo-Pythagoreans of Alexandria.

This conception of every doctrine as having two aspects, one exoteric and the other esoteric, apparently contradictory but in reality complementary, may be taken as a general rule since it corresponds with the nature of things as they are. Even when this distinction is not openly acknowledged, there exists of necessity in any doctrine of any depth at all something which corresponds to these two aspects, illustrated by such well known antitheses as outer and inner, the bone and the marrow, the visible and the occult, the wide road and the narrow, letter and spirit, the rind and the flesh. In Greece itself the doctrine of the philosophers had been preceded in the same way by the religious mysteries whose very name implies silence and secrecy. We know that the participants had to swear to say nothing of the secret rites which the liturgical drama of the famous nights of Eleusis would have revealed to them, and that they kept their oath without fail.

More generally the vow of silence concerning this kind of knowledge has different degrees according to the nature of the teaching. It may be silence imposed upon the postulants as a discipline designed to test their character, as was the custom of the

followers of Pythagoras; or to protect certain technical secrets relat-
ing to the practice of a trade, a science, or an art (all ancient profes-
sions come under such headings). Their practice required precise
qualifications and the knowledge of formulae which it was forbidden to divulge.

Passing now beyond the literal meaning we find that the obscurity of a doctrine may persist in spite of very clear and complete
explanations. In this case the esoteric aspect stems from the difference between minds and of the *de facto* inability to understand
on the part of the audience. Another kind of secret is attached
to the symbolic nature of all written or spoken expression, especially when it is a matter of spiritual teaching. There will always
remain something unsaid in all formulations of truth, since language is not adapted to conveying the imageless conceptions of
the mind. Finally and above all the true secret reveals itself as
such by its very nature and no one is capable of stating it. It
remains inexpressible and inaccessible to the profane mind and
can only be grasped by means of symbols. What the master transmits to the pupil is not the secret itself but the symbol and the
spiritual influence which will enable the student to grasp it himself.

So the notion of esoteric teaching contains within it three stages
or envelopes increasingly difficult to pass through. The secret or
mystery is first of all what must be received in silence and then
of which it is forbidden to speak and finally of which it is found
to be difficult to speak.

The first hurdle resides in the nature of all forms of expression
in language. This may be called an 'objective' esotericism. The
second barrier lies in the inadequate qualifications of the person
to whom the teaching is given. This may be called 'subjective'
esotericism. Finally, the last veil hiding the truth as we try to
express it is its own naturally inscrutable nature. This is 'essential' esotericism, or we may call it metaphysical, about which we
shall be speaking later for it is thanks to this that all traditional
doctrines are found to be interiorly one.

It needs to be added that although there is a logical correlation
between the exoteric and the esoteric aspects of any doctrine, there
is not an exact equivalence between them since the interior aspect
surpasses the exterior which it integrates into a larger whole, even
when the exterior aspect, as has happened in the West, has adopted
a religious form. Esotericism is not therefore merely the inner
aspect of a religion; for exotericism does not necessarily nor always
adopt a religious form nor has religion any monopoly of the sacred.
Nor is esotericism a special form of religion destined for the use

of a privileged few as has sometimes been supposed. In itself it is nothing since it is only a way of looking at sacred things which gives deeper insight. It enables one to grasp the inner meaning of all forms, be they religious or not. In religion, whilst not being exclusive, the social character is dominant. It has come into being for the sake of all, whereas esoteric understanding can only be achieved by some. This is not a matter of choice but a fact of nature. The secrets of esotericism become the mysteries of religion. Religion is an exteriorization of such doctrine as is necessary for the common salvation of men and women, this salvation being a deliverance limited to the plane of being. For religion is concerned with beings as individuals and as humans; it provides for them those psychic and spiritual conditions most compatible with this state, without endeavouring to free them from this state.

Certainly man as man cannot surpass himself, but if he can attain to that knowledge and deliverance which are one and the same thing, this is because he already has within him a universal nature corresponding to them. The esoteric teaching which as we shall see makes use of initiation as the method by which to reveal itself, has as its objective the freeing of man from the limitations of his earthly state and of activating the capacity with which he has been endowed of attaining to higher states of being in a way which is both active and irreversible, through the rigorous and exact performance of rites.

2.

The Three Worlds

As with all branches of knowledge esotericism has its own vocabulary and symbols. It has attached a precise meaning to the terms which it has borrowed from other disciplines. These means of expression date from the time when they were first accepted in use. So we must ask ourselves, to what world outlook, in the minds of their contemporary users and in the science of those ancient times, do they correspond?

The thinkers of antiquity assumed the existence of a higher world inhabited by invisible powers, above that of visible and sensible nature. They began with Man whom they naturally placed at the centre of the cosmos, and they divided the universe into a threefold entity consisting of a material world, a psychic or mental world, and a spiritual world. This hierarchical order remained as the basis of instruction up to medieval times. The central and mediating role assigned to man in the cosmos may be explained by the identity of the elements which compose both one and the other. The Pythagoreans taught that man is a microcosm, a little world, a doctrine adopted by Plato and retained by thinkers down to the Middle Ages. This analogy harmoniously united the world and man, the macrocosm and the microcosm, and so enabled thinkers to distinguish in man three modes of existence. The material world corresponds to man's body, to the psychic world, his mind, and to the spiritual world, his soul. This threefold division gave rise to three branches of knowledge, the science of nature or physics, the science of the mind or psychology, and the science of the spiritual or metaphysics, so called because its domain extended beyond that of the physical or natural. Let us at once take note that the spiritual is not an individual faculty but a universal one which is related to the higher states of being.

The threefold division into spirit, mind, and body, which is so unfamiliar to us today, was common to all traditional doctrines, although the limits of their respective domains did not always coincide exactly. The same division is to be found in the Hindu and Chinese traditions. The Jewish tradition explicitly maintains this tripartite formula in Genesis, Chapter Two, where man is made 'a living soul' by the union of the body formed of the dust of the earth and the inbreathing of the spirit. Plato adopted it and after him the Latin-speaking philosophers translated the three Greek words *nous, psyche, soma* by the three Latin equivalents *spiritus, anima, corpus*.

The Christian tradition was heir to this threefold formula, included by John at the beginning of his Gospel, which is *the* source of Christian esotericism. *Verbum, Lux,* and *Vita,* these correspond to the three worlds, the spiritual, the psychic, and the material. It should be remembered that light corresponds to the psychic or subtle state which is that of all theophanies.

St Irenaeus clearly employs the same division in his treatise on the Resurrection: 'There are three principles in the perfect man: body, mind (soul), and spirit. The one which saves and shapes is the spirit. The one which is given unity and form is the body. Then, an intermediary between the two, there is the soul, or mind, which sometimes obeys the spirit and is raised up by it and sometimes condescends to the body and is degraded with earthly passions.' However, in order to avoid imputing to the mind an envelope in some way corporeal, the Christian theologians ended by making the mind and the spirit so nearly identical that they utterly confused the one with the other. This ultimately resulted in the famous Cartesian dualism, and also in the confusion of the psychic with the spiritual, which at the present time in so far they are accepted at all, are held to be identical. However, if the mind is the mediator between the higher and lower states of our being, there must exist a nature common to them all. It is for this reason that St Augustine and also St Bonaventure posited for the soul a subtle body, a traditional doctrine which St Thomas Aquinas discarded for fear of 'materializing' the mind.

3.

Intuition, Reason, and Intellect

In man the hierarchy of these three states corresponds to three faculties designed to understand them in a specific way. Sensible intuition for the body, imagination for the mind (or rather reason and imagination for the psycho-mental complex), and pure intellect or transcendent intuition for the spirit. Bodily intuition, mediated by the senses and imagination, does not present any problem, whereas the parallel between reason and intellect requires some explanation.

The esoteric outlook can only be accepted and understood by intellectual intuition or intellect which is the tool of the spirit, and is validated by interior evidence of causal relations which precedes all experiential knowledge. This is the particular approach of metaphysics and of the knowledge of those principles which are universal. Here we are entering a territory where there are no longer opposites, conflicts, complementarities, nor symmetries, because the intellect is active in the realm of unity, and an isomorphic continuity with all that really is. Aristotle said that intellect is truer than science and St Thomas Aquinas that it is the *habitus* of principles or the world of causes. In an even more demanding way Arab writers on the spiritual could affirm that 'The doctrine of Unity is unique and indivisible'. The metaphysical outlook by definition does not share in the relativity of reason, and this implies within its own realm complete certainty. On the other hand it is inexpressible and unimaginable and arises from concepts which can only be approached by means of symbols. This symbolic mode of expression in no way denies the reality of other orders of existence, but it places them in their proper order beneath it, thanks to the power of its secret wisdom. Platonic ideas, mathematical invariants, and the symbols of ancient arts are examples of what is subordinated on different levels of reality.

Modern science on the contrary has reason as its dialectical tool, bound up with language and applied to every objective. Its links with language enable it to respect the rules of logic and grammar but this does not imply any guarantee of certainty with regard to its conclusions and even less to its premises. For reason is only a purely deductive and discursive mode of thought, a *habitus conclusionum,* as the Scholastics would have it, which does not go back to ultimate causes. Reason is a network, whose mesh is moderately close, cast over the phenomenal world, and making contact with those phenomena which are sufficiently *dense,* but which allows those phenomena which are more subtle to slip through and ignores them. For science and reason non-observable and non-measurable events do not exist. This is even more true when it is a question of a different sort of reality. We must understand that reality cannot be equated with this gross form of treatment nor limited by such an inevitably provisional technique. The answer which reason gives us — and it is only an answer — is strictly dependent on the question asked; it is dependent on it as regards unity, measure, and scale. Every answer is to some extent implicit in the question, because of the presuppositions inherent in it. Thus the echo seems to be the model for every 'intelligent' answer as tautology is for all strict reasoning.

On the other hand, speech only acquires its profound meaning as the echo of a thought couched in the language of the past — i.e. symbolically — to evoke an ever-present reality which has become hidden from us under the progressive materialization of our understanding. Neither reason nor our experience can guarantee truth for us because our experience is entirely historical and human, and too short, too recent, too immature, too limited, in a universe which has known states very different from ours, which have nothing in common with what we know as experience. For our experience takes no account of the particular nature of our own times which would alone enable us to receive a direct witness, from the remotest ages, by which I mean learning from tradition.

4.

Tradition

We would do well to understand what is meant by the concept of tradition since it is usually denied, misrepresented, or misunderstood. It has nothing to do with local colour or popular customs nor with curious local activities collected by some students of folklore. It is concerned with origins: tradition is the handing on of a complex of established means of facilitating our understanding of the immanent principles of universal order, since it has not been given to mankind to understand unaided the meaning of his existence. The idea most nearly equivalent and most able to evoke the meaning of the word tradition would be that of the spiritual relationship between a master and a pupil. That is to say of a formative influence analogous to that of spiritual vocation or inspiration, as actual for the spirit as heredity is for the body. What we are concerned with here is an inner knowledge, coexistent with life itself; a coexistent reality, but at the same time an awareness of a superior consciousness, recognized as such, and at this level inseparable from the person it has brought to birth and for whom it constitutes their reason for existence.

From this point of view the person is completely what he transmits, he only is in what he transmits, and in the degree to which he *does* transmit. Independence and individuality are thus seen to be relative realities only, which bear witness to our progressive separation and continuous falling away from the possession of an all-embracing original wisdom, a wisdom which is quite compatible with an archaic way of life.

This original state can be equated with the concept of a primordial centre of which, in the Judaeo-Christian tradition, the Earthly Paradise is one of the symbols; with the proviso that we always recall that this state, this tradition, and this centre only constitute three expressions of the one reality. Thanks to this tradition, which antedates history, knowledge of principial truth has been, from the beginning, the common property of all humanity, and has subsequently been revealed in the highest and most perfect theological systems of the historic age. But a natural degeneration has given rise to specialization and obscuration which have resulted in an ever-increasing gap between the message, those who transmit it, and those who receive it. Some explanation became more and more necessary since a polarization occurred between the external literal aspect expressed in ritual and the original meaning, which became more and more hidden within and obscured, and so, hard to understand.

In the West this exterior aspect was generally expressed in religious terms. Intended for the general mass of the faithful, the doctrine split into three elements, dogma for the reason, morals for the mind, and rites and ceremonies for the body. During the time in which this split was taking place in the West, the deeper meaning became esoteric and was gradually reduced to greater and greater obscurity, so that now we are compelled to refer to parallel examples from Eastern spirituality to understand the coherence and validity of our own tradition.

The progressive lack of real understanding of the idea of tradition has for a long time past prevented us from grasping the true nature of ancient civilizations, both eastern and western, and at the same time has made it impossible for us to return to that inclusive point of view which they had. Only as we return to basic principles can we gain a comprehensive understanding without suppressing anything. This will enable us to make a breakthrough to a new use of language, restore our power to remember and facilitate our inventive faculties, and so establish links between the most seemingly diverse branches of knowledge. All this is only possible as we acknowledge the privileged centre as possessing an inexhaustibly rich store of possibilities which are mediated to us by means of symbols.

5.

Symbolism

Symbols, acting as a bridge between the corporeal and the mental, enable every intelligible concept to be accessible to us by means of our senses. They stand as mediators of the psychic realm and so possess a double nature which enables them to convey more than one meaning, and indeed many cohering interpretations which are equally true according to the point of view from which they are considered. They have within them a complex of inter-related ideas which are not susceptible to analytical treatment. Each one of us can interpret them at our own level. Symbols are more a means of revelation than they are of self-expression. The symbol is a genus of which the various examples such as words, signs, numbers, gestures, graphic representations, actions, and rites are the different species. Rational, logical, grammatical speech is tied to physical or literal meaning, whereas symbols, whether graphic or 'acted', are inclusive and intuitive. They present evocative emblems which are sufficiently imprecise to enable them to be interpreted in contradictory, albeit complementary ways. Moreover if we push the search for origins to its conclusion we find that the literal meaning itself relies on a symbol whose existence has long since been obscured by our habitually ignoring it.

The science of symbols is based on the correspondence which exists between the different orders of reality, the natural and the supernatural, the natural here being seen to be but the exteriorization of the supernatural. The golden rule of symbols is that reality of a certain order may be represented by reality of a lower order, but the reverse is impossible, since the symbol must always be more readily comprehensible than that which it symbolizes. This law derives from the need for the maintenance of cosmic balance at any given moment. A balance in which every part is in its proper relation to the whole. So the part may stand for the whole, the lower may witness to the higher and the known point to the unknown.

True symbolism is not arbitrary. It springs from Nature, which as the thinkers of the Middle Ages believed, can be taken as a symbol of a higher reality. The world seemed to them to speak a divine language, or as Berkeley put it, 'the language by which the infinite spirit communicates with finite intelligence'. The different realms of nature together provide the alphabet of symbolism. Grammar, mathematics and the other traditional sciences, arts and crafts are all brought into play as supports and means of expression of metaphysical knowledge, in addition to their own intrinsic value, but also *thanks to this intrinsic value.*

Every act can become an appropriate symbol. Even historical events bear witness to the laws which govern universal manifestation. This analogical way of thinking is based on that which relates the microcosm to the macrocosm through the identity of their elements and their energies.

Finally it should be said that in order that symbolism may be correctly understood, every symbol must be interpreted as a mirror image of reality, i.e. inversely, formally, and not merely with reference to its intrinsic meaning. The image in a mirror provides an inverted image of whatever it reflects, yet without distorting the object. Whatever is greatest or first in the principial order becomes the smallest and the last in the order of manifestation. What is within becomes external and *vice versa.* In short, symbolism is the key to the revealing of all secrets, the Ariadne's thread linking the different orders of reality. By means of it we reason, we dream, and to it we owe our existence, since heredity in every way is also a symbolic concept, as is the analogy between physical and psychic laws. All manifestation is a symbol of its begetter or of its cause. Thus symbolism is not, as is often thought, merely the poetic fancy of a literary school or a quality arbitrarily added to things. But it is the very stuff of reality itself which it strives to express by means of what in it is most essential and most hidden; its form, its rhythm, and its action. Symbolism is in truth a particular example of the universal science of rhythm if understood in the most comprehensive way possible. It is the creative act found at the origin of all manifestation, whether seen, heard, or experienced in life, and it is this that every traditional ritual claims to reproduce.

6.

Rite, Rhythm, and Act

Rhythm is hidden at the heart of all manifestation, it is part of every profound human activity — and indeed it is in everything that is, since nothing is totally inert. It shapes us as heredity controls the formation of human beings and our intellectual background the evolution of our thought. It is the regular framework of the whole of nature, of all existence from the material onwards. Man transforms rhythms and is transformed by them. From the cradle to the grave he is borne along on a stream of great moving waves, the great cycle of the years, seasons, and days determines the course of his life. Man is in love with rhythms and avidly seeks to uncover them. Through them he achieves the satisfaction of one of his basic needs, that of being in communication with the world around him, in harmony with nature, and at peace with himself.

The intellectual act we call comprehension or even knowing consists in recalling to mind something already known, by means of which we can envelope the new in the mantle of the familiar. We do this by means of an image or a rhythm common to both. The sensible object sets in motion a familiar reaction by means of which the feared and the unexpected become tolerable, accepted, and finally part of us. The new and the unexpected are subsumed in the magic of the rhythm of the familiar.

The essential character of rhythm lies in its dual nature in which each phase complements the other, alternately succeeding one another, centred on a point of balance which is also their point of arrival and departure. This central point which the rhythm preserves is the creator of form because it serves to establish the most appropriate frequency and the one with the minimum expenditure of energy. The waves of this harmonious vibration are spread by a subtle correspondence beyond the physical world into the psychic realm where they produce that state of harmony and serenity necessary for the achievement of higher states of being. The two-phase nature of all rhythm is exemplified in the inhale and exhale of breathing and the diastole and systole of the heart, both of which are used in most rites designed to help the achievement of metaphysical realization.

Such rites consist of procedures which enable the individual participant to share in the collective power generated by every living tradition. Hindu *mantras* and Muslim *dhikrs* as well as sacred dances, hymns and chants, metrical prayers, and the prayer of the heart, are all examples; they put the body and soul of the individual *en rapport* with the collectivity of which they are a part, and also with the rhythm of the universe, which Plato called the music of the spheres. Every rite and every single act, performed correctly, bring about the transmutation of the subtle elements in the person and facilitate the recovery of that original state of wholeness which is the paradisal state. Rites are based on an intemporal conception of actions which take place in an eternal now where all can take place simultaneously. This will not be in any way verifiable by the methods of modern science but is proven nevertheless since an absolutely identical repetition implies 'action outside time' which alone can be accomplished by means of ritual.

7.

Initiation

Initiation, which is designed to introduce the aspirant to the way of personal realization, is, in its essence, the transmission of spiritual influences. This 'blessing' is conferred by a Master, himself an initiate, thanks to the uninterrupted chain, i.e. to the effective inheritance which unites him with the beginning of the chain, and its commencement in time. Every rite of initiation includes symbolic acts which give witness to its origin; for example, the kiss of the Master which transmits the 'breath' of spiritual influence, by which the world came into being. The Master in using such gestures is not acting as an individual, but as a link in the chain, as the transmitter of a power which is greater than he is, and of which he is only a humble servant.

To be effective, initiation requires three conditions on the part of the one who seeks it; a genuine aptitude, willingness to receive it in a legitimate form, and personal self-understanding. Moreover the postulant should possess certain physical, moral, and intellectual qualifications. He or she, while of course having limitations, should have such as will offer the least impediment to their development. Their objective is the active attainment of higher states of being, or if you wish, communion with the universal Self, the underlying principle of all states of being. All this requires perfect harmony in the soul, complete mastery of one's feelings, and a genuine balance between all the different facets of the personality. These demands at once exclude all who have a bodily defect or who are psychically unbalanced. Such weaknesses would inevitably be an obstacle on the arduous path the postulant wishes to tread, even if such defects are the result of an accident. For everything which happens to us has a certain corresponding feature within us, without which nothing could affect us. The conditions which are essential for the reception of initiation can be listed under four headings: bodily purity, nobility of feelings, wide intellectual horizons, and an exalted spiritual nature.

Initiation should be bestowed by a qualified master, known to the Hindus as a *guru* and to the Orthodox as a *geron* (both words meaning an old man). In Islam he is known as a *sheikh*. The master plays the part of spiritual father to the disciple, for initiation is a second birth, and he will be alongside him as he encounters difficulties in following the path. As for the necessary theoretical knowledge, each organization will have its own means of instruction.

Even when initiation has been received, it remains potential until it has been effectively actualized by personal effort under the guidance of that master who resides within each one of us. The aim of this effort is the realization of those higher states which develop our personality. This notion of higher states is so unfamiliar to most people today that a word of explanation is necessary. Every individual, even when considered from the viewpoint of the greatest extent of his capabilities, is not a total being, but only one particular state of manifestation of that being, occupying a set place in the infinite series of possible states which comprise a total being. For existence in its indivisible unity is comprised of an infinite number of modes of manifestation. This infinite multiplicity of states of being is equally applicable to any one being and every one of these states of being must be realized at a different level of existence.

For example the bodily part of me is only the physical mode of a particular individual and is only one limited state among a multitude of possible states of being. Existence itself in all its variety is only an example of what might be called one possibility of manifestation, whereas Universal Possibility following Leibniz as adapted by Guénon includes also the possibility of non-manifestation for which the concept of existence postulated by cosmology and the concept of being postulated by ontology are no longer sufficient. Universal Possibility is the concern of the true metaphysic.

If one prefers to use the Hindu terminology one could say that the I is only a particular and transitory aspect of the Self or of that which is the Transcendent Principle. This concept must be taken to include the three worlds and concerns not only individual states of manifestation dependent on form but those supra-individual subtle states, and even more states of non-manifestation or possible states which are contained in the Oneness of the Self, which are contained in the universal totality. This infinite multiplicity of states of being, which corresponds to the theological notion of divine omnipotence, is a fundamental metaphysical truth, and the highest concept which it is possible for the human mind to conceive.

If the manifestation of higher states can, by certain qualified persons, be conceived of as possible, this is because there is an analogy between the process of the formation of the world and the spiritual development of an individual, but in the opposite direction, since the development of the world implies multiplicity and spiritual development, is a return to principial unity.

From the universal point of view the world can be considered from three aspects: in a state of non-manifestation representing Universal Possibility, in a state of subtle formless manifestation representing the *Animus Mundi* or world-soul, and in a state of formal or material manifestation which is the world of matter and substance. The creation of the world can be seen as an ordering of chaos resulting from the issue of a divine order which in the Bible is represented by God's *Fiat Lux* since Light has always accompanied theophanies and is the concomitant of order. The heavenly shaft of this 'order' or 'spiritual influence' has given rise to a luminous vibration at the centre of the double chaos. This vibration separated the waters under the firmament from those above the firmament (Genesis 1: 6-7), i.e. separated the world of form from the subtle formless world, the manifest from the non-manifest, as described in the book of Genesis. The surface of the waters at their plane of separation represents the point at which the passage of the individual to the universal takes place; the level on which the heavenly ray of illumination shines.

For like the divine *Fiat Lux*, the spiritual influence transmitted in initiation to the postulant illuminates the dark chaos of his nature as an individual. This spark of the light of understanding shines out in all directions from the centre of being symbolized by the heart, and brings to perfection all the possibilities inherent in that person. This invisible action is portrayed in different traditions as the unfolding of a flower, the rose, or the lotus on the surface of water. Thus the cosmic rhythm transmitted by the original rite resonates in the life of the postulant, whose function henceforth is to follow and bring to perfection the divine plan. It is when he understands his ineluctable destiny that the future initiate becomes worthy of initiation, which is actualized through the development of the possibilities inherent in his nature; which is the locus of all mystery. As the celebrated Hindu dictum puts it: 'What is here is there and what is not here is nowhere.'

8.

The Centre and the Heart

All authentic transmission of spiritual influence originates from a centre which is linked by an unbroken chain to the primordial centre. Geographically speaking, certain places exist which are especially suitable for enhancing the efficacy of this influence. A very precise science of sacred geography determined the correct location of such sanctuaries, which subsequently were established there, and which are among the most famous of all historical sites. Delphi, Jerusalem, Rome, to mention some of those in the West. The attachment of temples to the primordial centre is symbolized by their ritual orientation and by the pilgrimages made to them, which for the pilgrims were in fact a return to the centre. From time immemorial mountains rendered sacred by theophanies represented for each tradition the centre of the world, as was Mount Meru for the Hindu tradition. On these mountains the first altars were erected and the first sacrifices were made. Stones and *betyles* raised in imitation of mountains were held to be dwelling places of the divine presence. An example of this is the Omphalos at Delphi, the spiritual centre of Greece and home of the Pythian prophetesses, a place imbued with the divine presence. Later the temples were concealed in the hearts of mountains in natural or artificial caves. This reversal of position and relationship between the mountain and the temple came about as a progressive obscuring of the tradition occurred and the sacred place was transformed into a subterranean site and the cave became the home of initiations and of mysteries.

There are as many of these sacred sites as there are traditions. They are all linked to a Holy Land, seat of the Primordial Tradition, the supreme land according to the Sanskrit word *Paradesha*, from which the Chaldeans derived their word *Pardes* and the Western word Paradise. This supreme Land is found in the different traditions under many different forms: a garden, a city, an island, a temple, a palace. As its origin is polar it is also the Pole or the World's Axis. It is also known as the Undefiled Country, the Land of Immortality, the Land of the Living, the Land of the Sun.

Geometrically considered as the origin of extension or biologically as the seed of light which by a rhythmic pulsation illuminates the whole of the manifest world, this Land, the Central Point, symbolizing a state of being, is the origin of the generation of all places, times, and states. In this supreme place where the heavenly ray of the influence from on high is reflected, all opposites are resolved and all contraries united. Point of departure and arrival, of beginning, of fulfilling, of principle and objective, it is the Unchanging Centre of Chinese philosophy, the Divine State of Islamic esoteric teaching, the Holy Palace of the Kabbala, or the divine presence of the Shekinah hidden in the Tabernacle.

The Primordial State corresponding to that of Paradise is that of Adam and Eve in the Garden of Paradise, the first stage in the realization of all higher states.

The essential attribute of such centres, which corresponds to the physical equilibrium of matter and energy or to the well-balanced mind, is the Peace of the Spirit; the Great Peace of Islam, the Deep Peace of the Rosicrucians, that *Pax* inscribed on the entrance of every Benedictine monastery. A Chinese text says: 'If the true cause of all is invisible and beyond our comprehension, only the spirit in a state of perfect simplicity can attain to it through a state of profound contemplation in the centre where all opposites are reconciled, and all is in a state of perfect balance.'

This true understanding is only possible because, to use a phrase of Aristotle, it is an identification, an isomorphism, as one might say today. Such an identification with Truth would be impossible if man were not more than he appears, the 'more' being provided by the unchanging Principle which is his essence and which tradition locates in the heart.

For if indirect and discursive knowledge depends on the reasoning mind, direct intuitive understanding depending on the attainment of higher states depends on 'the knowing heart'. This 'knowing heart' is not an individual possession but is a universal property, as is what is known by it. From the point of view of the microcosm, all traditions locate the centre of being in 'the cavern of the heart'. The heart is the organ of understanding, whereas the vehicle of spiritual love is the breath of the spirit, the *Pneuma* through its links with life. In the heart is hidden the divine indestructible principle which the Hebrew tradition calls *luz*. According to the Chinese this is the embryo of the immortal one to which the soul remains attached for some time after death.

The Hindu Tantric rites reveal better than any other that the work of initiation is a work of transformation achieved by the impalpable reabsorption of the subtle energies through the centres (or *chakras*) of the body. These *chakras* are located along the spinal cord at points incapable of precise localization but linked to the whole body by the mysterious power of the nerves and of the blood. This energy comes to the 'command centre' located in the forehead between the eyes. This centre is related to the 'sense of eternity' and the invisible eye of knowledge. It is here that we receive instruction from our inner master, identical with the Hindu *atma* and of the Self which is the primordial and most general form of the Universal Principle which we may call the spirit. Through this Spirit we are able to attain to the perfection of our human state before transcending it.

9.

The Greater and the Lesser Mysteries

The stages of initiation are a varying hierarchy of degrees for which it is convenient to borrow the terminology used in the mysteries of antiquity because it is capable of being generally applied. We, with them, make a distinction between the Lesser and the Greater Mysteries and make use of the term Adept (*Epoptes*); these comprise the three stages of all initiation.

The Lesser mysteries were designed to show the aspirants the laws of becoming which govern the cosmos and to restore the primordial state of being, and they were a preparation for initiation into the Greater mysteries which are concerned only with the metaphysical realm. They put special emphasis on rites of purification by actions, sometimes called journeys or tests. The aspirant has to be restored to a state of simplicity comparable to that of a child, the *prima materia* of alchemy, thus rendering him capable of receiving the illumination of initiation which was to follow. The spiritual influence conveying this illumination should not encounter any obstacle due to earlier discordant elements in the personality. In the language of the Kabbalah this purification corresponds to 'the stripping of the bark', and in Masonic terms to 'the refinement of the metal', the bark and the metal symbolizing the residues of those previous psychic states which must be transcended. The first tests enable the initiate to be liberated from the domain of the senses, but for all that remaining in the realm of nature. According to a geometrical symbolism borrowed from Islam, this first liberation frees the person horizontally, providing 'extension', and by so doing restores the state of the Primordial Man or True Man of Taoism. The individual retains his human nature but is liberated in the spirit from time and the Ten Thousand Things, the Taoist name for the manifest world.

The fully spiritual objectives and the realization of higher formless states, both conditioned and unconditioned, are the proper concern of the Greater mysteries. The consummation of this process is deliverance from the world of manifestation and the attainment of Principial Union, that state to which different traditions have given different names: the Beatific Vision, the Light of Glory, the Supreme Identity. The development of the second stage is symbolized as being a vertical exaltation (or ascension) to that state which Islam calls the Universal Man and Taoism the Transcendent Man. The fulfilment of the process within nature gives rise to the Primordial Man, whereas the Universal Man may be identical with the principle of universal manifestation itself.

If it is asked how can the pretension to be in communication with higher states of being be justified, it may be pointed out that in fact this is the taking possession of a precious inner treasure which is part of the potentiality of every person so endowed. Furthermore, the achievement of these states is validated by the existence of corresponding gifts, generally referred to as revelation and inspiration. That which appears outwardly as revelation is manifested inwardly as inspiration. The effective means of realization of such states follows on two preliminaries, detachment and concentration; concentration is impossible without prior detachment.

Let us return to the ancient mysteries which provide interesting insights into the process of initiation. The postulant undertook a prolonged fast before he was subjected to purification by the elements, which he submitted to naked and in silence. The tests took the form of successive journeys, each one of which was related to one of the elements of nature, an underground journey, a journey on water, and finally in the air by an ascent into heaven. The subterranean exploration was seen as a descent into the Infernal Regions, i.e. into the inferior states of being. The meaning of this *katabasis* was understood to be the recapitulation of earlier states of being which permitted the postulant to exhaust his inferior potentialities before rising to subsequent higher states. Initiation was thought of as a second birth, the descent into the lower world symbolized a death to the profane world. As with every transformation, this one also occurred in darkness and the postulant received a new name representing his new nature. Death and rebirth were two complementary phases of the one change, seen from opposite sides.

Since the second birth takes place in the psychic domain it is here also that the first steps of the initiatic process will occur. The crucial stage which marks the turning point is the moment of transition from the domain of the psychic to that of the spirit, and this change was the concern of the Greater mysteries. Here was a third birth by which one was liberated from attachment to the cosmos, it was symbolized by the emergence from the cavern. In the mysteries of Eleusis final union with the divine was symbolized by a sacred marriage celebrated between the hierophant and the goddess personified by a priestess. The fruit of this union was given the name of the postulant himself and was henceforth adopted into the family of the 'the sons of heaven and earth', as we read in the Orphic fragments. One year later the postulants could claim the rank of *epopt*, i.e. a mystic or an Adept. This formal recognition confirmed their permanent union with the divinity.

10.

The Three Ways: Castes and Callings

Plotinus has pointed out that every individual on his journey back to his heavenly home starts out on his own particular path. At the start there is an infinity of separate paths. 'But this multiplicity of paths, which is both necessary and natural, does not fly in the face of doctrinal unity. The individual paths eventually come together since they are linked by a common function and nature. The Hindu tradition in its essence distinguishes three principal ways (*margas*), the way of action (*karma*), the way of devotion (*bakhti*), and the way of knowledge (*jnana*). In practice these may be reduced to two since the first two relate to the Lesser mysteries and to royal initiation and the last to the Greater mysteries and to sacerdotal initiation. A natural correspondence between these three ways and the three main Hindu Castes exists which should not be seen as applicable only to India. In every society a distinction analogous to that of Hindu castes may be found since they express different fundamental functions which must be fulfilled in every society no matter where it exists. A function of teaching and informing, which in India is under the authority of the Brahmins; a function of control and the administration of justice, which is the function of the noble warriors (*kshatriya*), which is also that of royal power; and finally an economic function involving money and trade, which is the function of the caste of merchants and artisans (*vaishya*); the craft initiation ceremonies were found in this caste.

It is noteworthy that in ancient Rome the god Janus (identical with the Hindu *Ganesha*), besides being the patron of the trade corporations, also presided over the mysteries. His essential attributes were symbolized by his holding a gold and a silver key, denoting spiritual and temporal sovreignty. The golden key was that of the sacerdotal initiation of the Greater mysteries and the silver one the kingly initiation of the Lesser mysteries. It was by virtue of his being the master of the seasons that Janus possessed these attributes because of the link which unites work to the rhythm of the passage of time, since originally work was on the land and was controlled by the changing seasons. This throws light on the famous episode of Demeter silently holding up an ear of corn before the students of the mysteries. So Janus opened and closed the cycle of the seasons, today one of the most awesome prerogatives of the Papacy, who are the heirs of the two symbolic keys. This is why the Guilds celebrated the feasts of the winter and summer solstice in honour of Janus. These two feasts are today celebrated by the feasts of the two St Johns at the same times. Both the work of agriculture and every art and craft can be the vehicle of realization for man as he lives in time. We find here one more example of the correspondence between individual self-realization and the development of the world. This correspondence was at the heart of all ancient intiation. All activities which affect the exterior world, provided they derive from the principles of the cosmos and are transformed into a spiritual act, can become a ritual capable of profound repercussions in the person performing it. For him it is the best means and sometimes the only means of effectively participating in his own tradition.

Seen thus, all work becomes a priesthood and a vocation in the true sense of that word which is 'a calling'. It is the performing by each person of an activity suitable to his particular gifts and one which can serve as a basis for his initiation since it accords with his individual talents. The individual's capacity for initiation is thus merged with his professional qualifications.

But initiation which takes one's work as its base will also affect the doing of that work. Work done as a vocation becomes the area in which understanding is applied, an understanding which is both complete and symbolic. Such work can produce a masterpiece, to use that word in its full sense of meaning a formal work produced by an accepted craftsman as the end of his apprenticeship.

In India one's function in society depended on hereditary qualifications. The caste system, which is founded on a deep understanding of human nature and its varying gifts, is liberating, and any errors in its application should not be allowed to detract from its value. The advantages are obvious. The caste system excludes competitiveness and unemployment, shares out work and guarantees its quality, making it easy and agreeable. By means of it the craftsman achieves a proficiency which seems almost second nature to him, and it assures the transmission of secret skills from father to son. The stability of the system is such that the only initiatic organizations known in the West both derive from craft organizations, namely the Guild system and Freemasonry, which were both in origin initiatory systems built on trades.

11.

Folk and Fairy Tales

In India at least, initiation was generally reserved for members of the first three castes. But it was necessary that those not eligible for this sort of initiation should have some means of access to their national traditions. This group included women, children, strangers, and those outside the caste system. The sacred doctrines transmitted orally have been handed down through the centuries in two different forms. A sacerdotal form preserved by the priesthood, as in the Bible or the Vedas, and in a popular form which right up to the present time has been transmitted orally by means of stories and legends whose symbolism has been so misunderstood. These legends do not contain as is often thought childish inventions but material, doctrinal in character, embodying the wisdom of past ages and preserved from distortion by their very obscurity. These narratives do not come, as a modern fashionable theory claims, from the *collective unconscious*, but they compose an *ancestral memory*, one might even say a *supramemory*. For this immanent memory is composed of the uncomprehended residue of an ancient awareness.

It is easy to recognize the initiatic themes which we have outlined, in the series of stories. In every tradition they refer to that which has been lost or hidden at some period or other. For example, the *soma* of the Hindus, the *haoma* of the Persians, the pronunciation of the divine name in Israel, the lost word of Masonry, the sacred vessel of the Graal legend, the hidden God of Isaiah, the Philosopher's Stone of the alchemists, the mythical Fountain of Youth, and even the Paradise Lost of the Bible. This last pinpoints the underlying meaning of them all as being that of a lost primordial state, a sense of eternity, a link with Tradition which must be restored, a truth which is rather concealed than lost. In some stories the hero must himself set out in search of an

unknown country, a hidden object or a lost fianceé. With supernatural help he succeeds in overcoming all difficulties and reaches
the end of his voyage, which has recapitulated the tests of the
initiatory process. The hero is usually a young man or the youngest of three brothers, or better still, a child, which reminds us
of the importance of the child in the mysteries. Sometimes, instead
of having to seek for a treasure or the lost beloved, the hero has
to find himself, and the transformation he undergoes is all the
more striking when he has been transformed into an animal, or
he may only have lost one member of his body or a faculty, usually
his voice, his sight or his intelligence, youth or beauty. Most tel-
ling of all, he is sometimes seeking for his heart or for light.

The hero is never left dependent on his own powers, he always
enjoys supernatural help, either fairies give him special powers
at birth or he is helped by powerful figures, or supernatural beings,
symbolizing spiritual influence. This influence is sometimes connected with a magical object, the Fountain of Youth, the *elixir
vitae*, or Water of Life and Death. But above all he is given power
over the three realms. In classical mythology this three-fold power
is represented by Hermes, with his wide-brimmed hat, his winged
staff or Caduceus, and wings on his heels. These three, in the royal
intiation referred to above, were transformed into the crown, the
sceptre, and the slippers, and in the knightly consecration, by the
helmet, the sword, and the spurs. In fairy and folk tales the modest
hero has to be content with the cap which makes him invisible,
the staff which makes him invincible, and the seven-league boots
which enable him to go wherever he wants.

In these stories there is often reference to the 'language of the
birds', knowledge of which reveals hidden secrets to the hero. This
language is strictly speaking that of poetry, the language of the
gods and the angels, bringing peace and reconciliation. Understanding the language of the birds means understanding the secrets
of nature which she herself reveals. Sigurd when he has overcome
the dragon, that is to say, the powers of the underworld, understands the language of the birds. The correspondence between
the age of the hero, the place where the action takes place, and
the wielders of power is noteworthy. Demons, snakes and all other
images of the underworld inhabit gloomy forests, the dwelling
place of aged sorcerers. The birds, on the other hand, welcome
one in gardens, the Garden of Eden, and are favourably disposed
towards the young.

We know that a death is the first and necessary step in all initiation. This dying is represented in a number of ways in these

stories. Firstly, a bodily death, in which case the hero is killed and cut to pieces, like Dionysus Zagreus, and a person endowed with the necessary powers resuscitates him in the flower of his youth. Or again, the hero is lost in the underworld, represented as a grotto, an underground palace, a sombre forest, the bottom of a lake or as Bluebeard's forbidden chamber, which all have the same symbolic meaning. In some cases death is replaced by a dethronement from high position, symbolized, for example, by the loss of an eye, i.e. of his intellectual powers.

Passing from the journey itself to the object for which it was undertaken, we find that this may be some marvellous object, such as Jason's Golden Fleece, Sir Perceval and the Graal, the Golden Apples, or the mystic Rose of the Beloved. This final stage on the quest may also take the form of an awakening, as in the case of the Sleeping Beauty, or a metamorphosis, like the Golden Ass of Apuleius. The final achievement of the state of union is often symbolized by winning the hand of the beloved, which explains the almost invariable standard ending in marriage, a true sacred union comparable with that of the initiate. Moreover, from our point of view, the most sophisticated of writing in recent centuries seems to have been a perversion of an authentic rite since it always tries to restore man's destiny to him. It is easy to determine what is ephemeral in a work, what dates it; it is its 'psychology', too involved in the social system of the time and its customs and history. What is indestructible and so remains, on the other hand, is the progress of the action, that is to say, the ritual aspect. The history of a man, his progress through life and his downfall through difficulties, this is the permanent subject matter of tales and romances. In some great works this element is particularly noticeable. The Odyssey, Pantagruel, the quest of the Graal, Dante's Divine Comedy, Shakespeare's plays, Goethe's Faust, which is derived from an ancient form of initiation used by Guilds. Wilhelm Meister uses the symbolism of the theatre, others that of a journey, of a voyage or of warfare.

In contrast to this sophisticated literature, popular stories do not use the symbolism of actions in a calculated way but directly. All principles are summed up in the action and at the same time any attempt at verisimilitude is avoided so that the sheer absurdity of the narrative reveals its symbolic significance more clearly. The evidence of this is so clear that if one denies this higher meaning to popular stories there is nothing left to give any point to the narrative. This is why popular tales reveal the supernatural to us in its purest state.

12.

The Intermediate Realm

The initiate on his path towards liberation has not so far encountered any major obstacles, nor has he any doubt as to the direction in which he must travel. The material world in all in its multiplicity and evident reality does not permit him to go far astray. Later on, when he reaches the world of formlessness, errors will no longer be possible. But this is not true when he encounters the region between the two, the intermediate world which is that of struggles, temptations, testing — in a word, the realm of duality. It is the domain of the psychic or subtle states of formless manifestation. The realm where one may encounter the extracorporeal survival of individuals who have died, the energies of non-human entities, the influence of the powers of the earth, the elemental spirits of Paracelsus which tradition calls gnomes, water sprites, sylphs, salamanders, djinns, demons, etc. These obscure forces, residues of long abandoned cults, mingle with authentic angelic powers and with wandering influences, as the Chinese call them, to constitute a strange, fascinating, and dangerous world.

On the other hand, although this world is that of struggle and change, it is also the world of illusion and beauty; it is in fact the world of the imaginary, the Hindu *Maya*. Here ideas take shape, languages become organized, influences are transmitted, and souls form unions. This world of perpetual change is illusory, like that of dreams. It is illusory in two ways, from the point of view of Principle, of which it is only a changing double, and from the point of view of the material world, which endows it with only a temporary form which maintains a provisional stability until its next transformation. This world is inevitable and necessary although its value is highly variable according to those beings who are manifest in it and who manifest it to us, for it is the meeting place of humanity and divine inspiration.

This intermediate world corresponds in celestial symbolism with the lowest part of the heavens, the sphere of the Moon, which is the first in the celestial series of spheres. Indian thought places the germ from which all creation sprang at the centre of this subtle world of mediation, often portrayed as the Cosmic Egg and its embryo the *Hiranyagharba* or golden embryo which is manifest in the form of a fiery globe of vibrating energy. This is its cosmic form; in the individual being this centre is found in the *pinda* (or subtle embryo).

Considered from the viewpoint of this centre of all things the transformations of the material world appear as a game played by Maya, a word which besides being translatable as 'illusion' can also mean art and measure because this 'illusion' is that by which man is measured. The creation of the world as it takes place in time is inevitably incomplete. Its completion is logically absurd and it is just this temporary nature that makes it an illusion. The cosmic realization of the divine imagination depletes and invalidates our temporal world. True creation is a perpetual flowing, like a river whose permanence is ensured by the ever-changing flow of water in it.

The human imagination, which derives its powers from the subtle energy of this intermediate world, is not a faculty to be treated with suspicion because it deceives us with fantasies. It is an autonomous psychic function, a means of union and an organ of perception. At one extreme imagination is our means of communication with the intermediate world, and at the other extreme it has that anticipatory function which we can use before acting in the material world. It presents all of us, and notably the artist, with the model for what is to be done. Its creativity puts us in touch by means of the energy of our spiritual vigour and the intention and application of the heart.

13.

Mysticism and Magic

The older a religion or a tradition is, the more multifarious and more complex is the picture of the intermediate world, as is exemplified by the exuberant mythologies of Egypt, India, and Greece. For the inheritors of these traditions there is danger in their heritage. For this intermediate world, more complex and more extensive than the material world, contains a chaotic variety of influences, amongst which whoever strives for self-realization risks permanent shipwreck. The same forces and the same phenomena can have directly opposite causes; Islamic doctrine underlines this in insisting that it is through the soul (*nefs*) which arises from the subtle intermediate world that Satan exercises his power over men. It is only at this level that he can become the adversary, a non-supreme God, because here we are in the realm of duality, whereas the Supreme Principal which is utterly transcendent and is identical with the Hindu unqualified Brahma is always unattainable.

So it is now appropriate that we should take a further step forward and distinguish the Hermetic path from other disciplines with which the reader might confuse it, notably magic and mysticism.

The common usage of the word mysticism implies a state of passivity, of supernatural grace whose involuntary arousal sometimes makes the understanding of its true nature difficult. The conception of mysticism as passive, however, does not do justice to the great Christian mystics accepted by the Church who, as the life of St John of the Cross demonstrates, reach very exalted states, by no means merely passive, and far above those reached by those initiates whose understanding has never been developed. The study of mystical theology on the contrary shows us that the spiritual experiences of the saints are exactly on a par with the *chaktas* of the East. The true difference is the absence in the case of a Christian mystic of an authentic line of transmission, thus leaving him isolated in his own tradition, whereas the oriental initiate is recognized, accepted, and given organized and legitimate support.

Magic is something altogether different. It is a traditional experimental science which has nothing to do with religion. All magical operations obey precise laws which the magician is constrained to obey. In order to do this he harnesses and makes use of the psychic forces available in the intermediate world. These subtle forces are linked to our bodily nature by two different means, the nervous system and the blood. Their effects are comparable to those of a magnetic field of force, which the magician uses for different purposes. In the material world these forces act through the mediation of subtle entities, such as the elementals in the natural realm and through certain objects or certain places. Magical action is based on the law of correspondence, which relates by affinity different elements in nature and transforms certain objects into *condensers* of energy. Sometimes as in India the magician concentrates these forces in his own body, thereby acquiring powers which go far beyond his ordinary capabilities. The condensation and dispersion of these subtle forces are comparable to the alchemical operations of coagulation and dissolution or those of ceremonial magic known as invocation and dismissal.

When these wandering influences are totally separated from the spiritual order, they fall into the domain of sorcery, which uses the most debased, indeed demonic forms of black magic. Among the most to be feared of such powers are those from which the spiritual element has been withdrawn and which have no physical connections. This is the explanation of the very harmful character of the residues of ancient religious beliefs and dead traditions; this is especially so when we are dealing with the so-called 'souls of the dead', the *doubles* of Egypt or the *ob* of the Jewish tradition, the Roman *manes* and even the *pretas* of India, since Gods no longer worshipped are debased to the level of demons. This confusion of anonymous metempsychoses in the intermediate world, this intermixture of obscure and awesome forces, explains the need for great understanding on the part of whoever is compelled to pass through this field of forces and to pass successfully various stages before reaching the heights, the truly spiritual levels which Muslim esoterism calls *stations*, i.e. firm and definitive states of being.

14.

Action, Love, and Beauty

The first two paths of initiation, those of action and devotion, comprising the Lesser mysteries, are virtually as inseparable as are body and soul, so that in fact their ways are one. The most holy of spiritually-minded persons would not survive for an hour if they abstained from all action. As Meister Eckhart said: 'There is no one in this life who attains a state which exempts him from work'. Action stems from that intent which unifies the succession of vague impulses experienced by the individual and overcomes interior anarchy by what Muhammed called 'the great and holy war' waged by the self against inner destructive urges. The object to which the original effort is directed is less important than its energy, its power, and its ardour. For right intention can redirect this force into the proper direction, just as *judo* redirects the blind impulsiveness of the opponent against himself. In the same way, in the Gospel parable, the clear-sighted paralytic leads the active blind man, or the master of the chariot directs the charioteer.

In the perfect act its author is transformed as much if not more than its object or its adversary. 'Every soul is the hostage of its acts', says the Q'uran, and tradition adds: 'To each shall be given that to which he inclines'. Each act is only an intermittent sign of a permanent intention to achieve an end which surpasses it. In the scholastic language of Thomas Aquinas: 'No active power can have any effect on any potential state of being which it has not been ordained to achieve'. That is to say that any action can only become the path of initiation if it is an authentic mode of being and if it is the result of a providential vocation, reinforced by the will of the person concerned. This inner warfare of the individual self with the supreme self is magnificently described in the sacred book of India, the *Bhagavad Gita*, in the dialogue

between Krishna and Arjuna in their chariot of war. The war here
referred to is an historical battle, a conflict between cosmic powers,
and the inner struggle in every individual. Krishna is the Self and
Arjuna the individual ego. Arjuna weakens when confronted with
the fratricidal war in which he must engage; he is not resigned
to attacking his own kith and kin. But Krishna points out to him
that to refrain would be to forfeit his vocation and his honour
and that doing so would solve nothing. 'The man who can see
action in inaction and inaction in action is the wise man', Krishna
tells him, and adds: 'Knowledge is more valuable than self-denial
(or action against oneself), but contemplation is more valuable
than knowledge, and detachment is to be preferred to contemplation'. This is because renouncing the fruits of one's action gives
peace of mind, and this is the true end of the path of initiation.
Detachment leads on to the way of spiritual devotion and 'pure
love'.

For the way of action leading to the living god is a way of love.
This can and should, by an analogical transposition, mean much
more than the call to the human sentiment it usually refers to.
It is in fact supra-individual and reveals itself as something as
profound as intellectual understanding. It foreshadows the union
of the being with its cause. Intellectual understanding being the
most disinterested form of love, their aim is the same, namely
a union which abolishes the distinction between myself and the
other. This reveals the inner meaning of the Hindu *Agni*, primordial fire, mediator between men and gods, in its twofold aspect
of the light of understanding and the warmth of love. For an understanding divorced from all feeling, which did not grasp that the
divine essence is only accessible to us under its guise of charity
and beauty, would render divine love incomprehensible. Love
forms the bridge between understanding and acting — beauty,
which is the pre-eminent characteristic of the world of images.
It is through the beautiful that understanding communicates most
easily with love, and the paths of action, devotion, and understanding are united by it.

All poetry of initiation, and this is especially true of Sufi poetry,
is a hymn to the beauty of the world, which is a reflection of the
divine beauty. The Persian poet Jami, speaking of this divine beauty,
says: 'Every loving heart, whether it knows it or not, is in love
with it. It is both the hidden treasure and the casket in which
it is concealed . . . Drink from the cup of appearances if you wish
to savour the elixir of eternal life.' Thus the Persian poets are only
repeating the teachings of other traditions as expressed in the *Vedas*

or by Pythagoras, Plato, and Denys the Areopagite, all of whom praise the power of beauty to evoke the divine. In all traditions of chivalry which rely on action, the feminine aspect of the Principial Unity is in evidence. It may be represented by such personification of energies as Wisdom, Power, Beauty. It may take as its manifestation some aspect of divinity as the *Shekinah* of Jewish tradition, or the Hindu *Shakti*. Or more simply, it may take the form of a feminine inspiration personified as 'La Madonna Intelligenzia' of Dio Compagni, or Ibn Arabi's Nizam, or Dante's Beatrice.

On the frontiers of the intermediate world and the formless world of the spirit, the beauty of the world of Imagination is revealed as a centre of exchange, an ideal model for human art, an attribute of the cosmos and the Divine Name. 'It is God alone whom we love in the beauty of the creation', said Ibn Arabi. It is this quality of beauty in every beloved that is seen by the lover, but it is entirely a manifestation by reflection of the divine attributes. Courtly love proclaims that contemplation of God in the feminine form is the most perfect for it is the motive for all action and the foundation of all worthy behaviour. The feeling appropriate to it is *le gai savoir*, which is that state of grace we enjoy when we embrace the world with enthusiasm, intoxicated by its beauty. It is the secret of the *Fedeli d'Amore* of Dante, and also of the Persian initiates in whom the feeling for beauty becomes a creative force arousing in men's souls a love for the divine compared with which all human love is but a pale reflexion.

God is no longer a Being infinitely remote but the merciful Friend, revealing himself to us as having a longing equal to our own, as a soul in search of our love, as we are for his. This is the meaning of the verse in the Q'uran reporting the words of Allah: 'I am a hidden treasure and have desired to be revealed'. So on the path of initiation, at this stage the search for knowledge needs the motive power of love. The concentration of all the faculties in the heart allows them to be used together, thus avoiding the mortal danger of intellectual abstraction. The intellect becomes in love with truth and love becomes the intelligence of the heart, or as the Sufis put it, 'love is transformed into the understanding heart'. As love is the secret of the lover, so also it is the most exact and unambiguous symbol of esoteric truth. To quote the words of another Persian mystic, Jalal-ud-Din Rumi, 'Reason which explains love is like an ass rolling in the mud. Only love can explain love.'

15.

The Great Peace: the Prayer of the Heart

From the state represented by the Primordial Man onwards the ways of action and love unite in the way of contemplation, which becomes the way of childlike simplicity and peace. The Jewish rite of the Sabbath will help us to understand this peace. The Sabbath is the only solemn rite instituted by the Jewish Tables of the Law or Ten Commandments. It forbids all action on the Sabbath even of the most trivial nature, such as collecting wood, lighting a fire, or picking a flower. For Talmudic tradition does not stress the degree of effort involved in the action, but rather the interference in the cosmic balance caused by the small change in the world brought about by human acts. Such an interference is a violation of the covenant relationship between God and his people. This is an exact counterpart of the Hindu notion of non-interference and the Taoist notion of non-action, and also the Profound Peace of the Rosicrucians. Man distances himself for a period from the unending flux of nature and is thus liberated from time. He is restored to his primordial or primal state of harmony with his environment, with plants and animals, that paradisal state he enjoyed in the Garden of Eden before the Fall. So the Sabbath is a return to Principial Unity and at the same time a foretaste of the Messianic Age when swords shall be beaten into ploughshares and spears into pruning-hooks, and the lion shall lie down with the lamb.

On the Sabbath the only permitted activity is that of prayer, which is the highest form of action beyond that of the performance of any task, and leading to the realization of a spiritual state. Prayer is the way of access to this state. What assists us in prayer is our intention, which is reinforced in most traditions by a ritually ordained physical direction for prayer.

The simplest prayer consists in the invocation of the Divine

Name, which brings an awareness of the Absolute, a union of heart and mind which purifies the mind, brings peace, and opens the spirit to the heavenly powers. All work of initiation should be done in the Name of the spiritual principle which is its origin. All rites, if they are to be valid, should begin with the invocation of this Name, above all in 'the prayer of the heart' as it is understood in Hesychastic, Buddhist, and Sufi prayers.

A primary mode of prayer is that which seeks a favour, and its efficacy depends in part on the traditional whole of which the supplicant is a member. For all such groups possess in addition to their material power a psychic capacity related to their members living and dead. This power is greater in those communities which are oldest and have the most members. Everyone can make use of this power by putting himself in harmony with his surroundings and by observing the prescribed rites. Every prayer prayed under these conditions will be to the spirit which animates the whole and which can be called its god. The efficacy of such prayer is conditional on a spiritual presence summoned by the invocation of the Name, and this presence may be represented by the master or teacher, especially when the disciple is alone. If it is deemed necessary for a number of people to be present, as in Masonic rites, the congregation may take the place of the master. The Kabbala teaches that when the sages discuss divine matters, the *Shekinah* or divine presence is invisibly present among them. It is essential that this spiritual influence should be concentrated in a building, such as a temple, or in an object, such as a relic, or as it was for the Hebrews, in the Ark of the Covenant.

God visits the hearts of the faithful in whatever form they expect him. It would be absurd to imagine that by prayer we can grasp the ultimate divine reality. 'Each one of us', says Ibn Arabi, 'prays to his own Lord, there is no prayer more exalted.'

At a higher level prayer is no longer a request but an aspiration of the finite towards the infinite, with the intention of obtaining the inner illumination which is the first step on the path to effective initiation. Although such prayer is interior, it can be exteriorized by means of words and gestures which create rhythmical vibrations which are echoed in the higher states. The object of such incantations is to achieve the status of the Universal Man by this communication with the totality of differing states. This prayer of the heart can continue when the mind is engaged on other matters; St Anthony remarked that prayer only reached perfection when one no longer realized one was praying.

A close connection exists between praying and the enlightenment it seeks. As we pray, our prayers return to us as enlightenment. The whole of creation itself may be seen as an aspiring
prayer, breathed by the creator, revealed to us in created light, cosmic light, the gift of life whose principle is the vibration of the
creative prayer. This response is our 'way of being'. 'Each one of
us knows how to pray and praise in his own appropriate way',
says the Q'uran. Five centuries earlier Proclus enunciated the same
truth when he said 'Every being prays according to the place he
occupies in nature'. We know that the worshipper may sometimes
think that he is not heard, that he obtains no answer. The reason
for this is that he does not yet understand that he is his own answer.
Prayer is an interior monologue, an outpouring by means of which
man gathers strength from the Universal Self. As Ibn Arabi says:
'It is the One who speaks and who listens'. Divine love is a sentiment which unites two beings in a closed circuit. Al Hallaj cried:
'Come unto me and give thanks to yourself'. In God there is no
other, or as Eckhart said, between God and Man there is no
between. The conversation is a silent dialogue between the believer
and the divine Name he invokes within him. 'I am known by you
alone and you exist by Me alone', said the Lord to his faithful friend,
to which Ibn Arabi replied: 'Where I deny knowing him, it is He
alone who recognizes me. When I know Him, there is He revealed in me.'

16.

Places and States

The changes undergone by our nature in the course of its inner development are innumerable and consist of an equal number of moments of awareness, which are all united in perfect simultaneity in the Self. The generally recognized stages of initiation only correspond in a general way with the principal steps in change. This visible gradation can only distinguish between differing functions and does not reflect the true invisible series of stages or steps. Besides, all these stages remain potential unless they are realized. As the Sufis say: 'The stations only exist for those who take up their position in them'. From this point of view we may describe initiation as a 'lived metaphysic', and its development is proportional to the degree to which the initiate is aware of it in his heart.

The different stages of initiation are represented by symbols of place, such as the series of heavens, but it should be understood that these different heavens represent in essence different states, as do all other places. We have already mentioned a first distinction between the Lesser and the Greater mysteries. The path which links them — and separates them — takes a long time to travel. Taoism recognizes three stages: that of the Wise Man (the acceptable postulant), the Man of Talent (the man on the way to enlightenment), and the True Man (the Primordial Man of Islamic teaching). Other traditions speak of seven stages which agree with the seven heavens; yet others reckon there are twelve. In the Middle Ages one of the seven liberal arts was associated with each of the seven heavens, the study of that art facilitating the realization of the particular stage involved with that heaven.

From the point of view of the microcosm we can establish a link between this system and the six subtle centres, or *chakras*, also called wheels or lotuses, of Tantric Buddhism, which are located along the length of the spinal cord in man. These lotuses represent forms of awareness born of cosmic energy in its luminous and sonorous form. The gradual development of these centres in men assisted by rites gives them certain powers (*siddhi*) and eventually brings about the total realization of their being. This sixfold division can also be equated with the six stages of the *sephiroth* in the Hebrew tradition.

Nevertheless, it must be admitted that it is impossible to make an exact comparison between the different supra-individual states as taught by the different traditions. What one can say is that these differing entities all fulfill the same symbolic functions; that of being mediators, and that they represent provisional stages, or in some cases optional. They are comparable to aeons, powers, perfections, the gods (or *divas*) of the Hindus, the angels of the Christian tradition, Platonic ideas, the demons and gods of the Greeks, the Jewish *sephiroth*, the uncreated energy of the Orthodox Christians, the divine Names in Islam. All are in effect divine attributes, whether personified or not, powers which occupy the distance which separates Primordial Man from Universal Man. These entities are attributes of the Principal Unity and not independent beings as idolatry implies, its error being to mistake the symbol for what it symbolizes.

The most important step, the turning point is to be found at the completion of the Lesser and at the commencement of the Greater mysteries. It is the terminal stage of Primordial Man, Adam in Eden. From here on a third birth enables the initiate to pass from the psychic to the spiritual world. He leaves the world of subtle manifestation to undergo a transformation, that is to say, a transition into the formless realm. It is evident that from this point onwards the steps of the Greater mysteries are only capable of description by symbols. For from the human point of view the True Man, the final stage of individual development in the intermediate world, cannot be distinguished from the Universal Man into which he has been divinely transformed, except by those who have reached the same higher stage, that of the True Man himself. The limitations of perspective inherent in the human state, stand in the way of an exact discernment of the various stages of ascent. For the ordinary man higher states become confused as he projects them on that central point where our mortal world is touched by the Divine light. The Transcendent Man can only reveal himself to us under the appearance of Primordial Man since he cannot discard his humanity.

The greatest of the Islamic Sheikhs, Ibn Arabi, has drawn from

a *surah* of the Q'uran nine categories of initiates, of which the
fifth is the most interesting as it is concerned with 'those who
bow the head', that is to say, those initiates who conceal themselves in the garments of humility and poverty. They are called
the *malamatiya* or the blameworthy, i.e. those who attract blame
from the profane world because they do not separate themselves
from the common people whose language and customs they adopt,
like the early Rosicrucians.

The true elite, even though they no longer exist, find a reflection in the minds of the common people. For it is such people
who have preserved most accurately and over the longest period
of time the hidden truths concealed in popular stories and legends.
In the same way it is the trade guilds which have suffered the
least from decay. It is said in Taoism that the Immortals appear
hidden under the guise of extravagant and vulgar figures, thus
providing themselves with a powerful defence against idle curiosity.

Once the supra-individual states have been achieved, no further mistakes can be made. The intermediate world vanishes when
an individual reaches the innermost heart of his being where the
invisible teacher holds sway, that teacher for whom the earthly
guru is merely a substitute. The two traditions in which the symbolism of superior states is most in evidence are Islam and Orthodox Christianity. In Islam the ladder of initiation is that of the
Poles and the Divine Names, of which there are an infinite number
which represents attributes or mediating qualities by which the
ladder can be mounted.

In Orthodoxy, God, who is in essence unreachable, communicates himself to us through his Energies, which are the graces
he gives us. His powers are as innumerable as the Divine Names
of which they are the active counterparts, Wisdom, Life, Power,
Truth, Justice, Love. In God his Being and his Act are one, as are
all the paths and all the names since they are all comprised in
his Absolute Potentiality.

Ibn Arabi dared to say: 'God is only a sign for the one who
understands the allusion'. Nevertheless we must grasp the irreversible nature of the analogy: when the Master announces 'Your
God is your Mirror and you are His Mirror' we must understand
that the relationship must be rigorously respected. You reflect God
and never should we think that God reflects us. To say the latter
would be a blasphemous lie. Logic demands that every reality has
its limits, which are its truth and the boundary beyond which
it is neither real nor true. For at this level the action, the actor,
and the awareness are one.

17.

Qualified Time: Cycles

Up to now we have considered the individual and his development without taking the times in which he lives into account.
But initiation is based on the whole man as he is at a certain
moment in time in a certain cosmic environment which is continuously interacting with the human order. The nature of man
does not solely depend on his personal qualities, which are the
active component in him, but also on his surroundings, which
are the passive element. These may either favour or inhibit his
growth. Moreover, the heredity of the person in question is a deter-
mining factor in that it encourages him to adopt those psychic
or physical elements in him which are naturally available to him
in his environment.

The heavenly planetary motions have always been symbols of
the different states of being because they draw together those
higher cosmic influences whose origin is immaterial and which
act continuously on us. Astrology does not, as has sometimes been
said, decide our human destiny. It only reveals the state of the
cosmos at the moment of our birth, in accordance with the harmony which exists increasingly between the different planes of
the world, and without which the world could not continue to
exist. The real decision comes from the individual himself; the
stars are only simple, legible, and unchanging signs which by his
interpretation of them help him to discern his destiny. At every
moment the whole world is in a state of balance, which makes
the concept of an analogical relationship between the microcosm
and the macrocosm reasonable. But this balance is not static but
moving and changing, and it is this perpetual motion that maintains the balance.

The stars as they move in their orbits reveal a motion which
it is possible to measure with great exactitude. Their periodic return

enables us to predict their future position exactly, and this prediction transposed into the psychic order can provide predictions which seem to surpass the achievements of reason, though this is not in reality the case. This periodic return of the planets and their cyclical movement has enabled us to use them analogically to describe the different states of being and to consider each of their differing movements as a different state. In the course of their common cyclical development, both man and the created world have followed the same path, a path which of necessity has taken them farther and farther from their source and their centre. It has traced a curve which we may call 'descending', which has distanced them more and more from the spiritual pole as they draw nearer to the pole of matter. This descent can thus be described as a progressive materialization or solidification; absolute materialization being the ultimate though forever unattainable end of such a path. During the course of this descent, which can also be thought of as a regression, mankind has lost the use of those spiritual faculties which once enabled him to have access to the suprasensible realms. In this regression man did not merely remain a spectator but has become an accomplice. In the end he has denied the existence of these higher realities which are hidden from the eyes of those who see without believing, for one can only see what one has previously imagined to be possible.

It is the Hindu tradition which has dealt most explicitly with the doctrine of Cosmic Cycles. It is not our intention to explain it in detail here, but we may say that the longest period conceived of by Hindu teaching is the *para* or 'Life of Brahma', which lasts for one hundred 'years of Brahma' and which is terminated by a universal dissolution. Each day of such a year is called a *kalpa* and represents the cycle of a world from its creation to its dissolution. Each *kalpa* or day of Brahma is divided into fourteen *manvantara* or 'era of *Manu*', Manu being a name for the cosmic intelligence who sets out the particular *dharma* or law for each era.

In its turn, each *manvantara* is divided into seventy-one *mahayuga*, and each *mahayuga* into four *yuga* whose length follow the proportions of 4, 3, 2, 1, with the result that the final *yuga* lasts one tenth of the whole. In order to have an idea of the scale of these periods in our time scale, the final *yuga*, one tenth of the whole, lasts 6480 of our years.

Since time is not mere vacuity but only exists with reference to what happens in it, each epoch is conditioned by the events by which it is manifested, events which, as the falling away from the primordial centre increases, occur with ever-increasing rapidity.

Materialism is thus increased by an acceleration, the speed of which reveals itself as the sense of an ever-increasing rush, by which history and every human activity, down to the most trivial parts of it, are oppressed. The need for initiation stems from these conditions of the modern world themselves and from the ever-increasing difficulties which confront those who wish to restore the situation, even for the lone individual. If a certain popular interest in esoteric matters is not to be condemned today, it is because it is the inevitable reaction which is always needed to maintain the balance of the cosmos between the poles of the spiritual and the material.

The passing from one cycle to another, of one *manvantara* to the next, for example, is brought about by an instantaneous restoration of balance which is spiritual and unknowable. The primordial tradition which has been more and more ignored is absorbed in an obscurity during which the change-over from one cycle to another takes place. This period of transition is accompanied by a cosmic cataclysm. This transformation destroys the ancient world and brings to birth the new world, a world obedient to the same Principle but not to the same secondary laws. The obligatory nature of this new awareness of the Principle, and of this clear-sightedness and new sincerity, is a truly traditional characteristic, which both provokes and justifies the emergence of a new world.

18.

The Supreme Identity and the Eternal Avatar

The motivation of all spiritual endeavour lies in the concern, which every individual has, about the means of ensuring for himself a favourable destiny after death. All the traditions insist on the difference of the posthumous states which await the profane and the initiated. There is nothing arbitrary about this difference; it is based on an inexorable logic by which man's deeds in this life, his habitual thoughts, and everything which has been his constant preoccupation, ineluctably determine his state after death. The psychic path of the soul freed from the body is determined by its effective virtues, by the level of understanding and by its spiritual function. Each soul after death will encounter those things which it has most ardently desired in this life. Its 'punishment' will consist justly in the realization that it had not known how to choose wisely and that it had aimed too low. In order to understand better the nature of this crucial moment at which the soul leaves the world of forms and reaches the formless world where it must identify itself with supra-individual entity, we should pause at the point where return is possible and where the individual is offered a number of alternatives. Ancient traditions locate this turning point of the cosmos in the Moon, the limit of the world of forms. The Moon, as we have already remarked, is the domain of the *Hiranyagarbha* (the golden embryo and the germ in the Cosmic Egg), the individual's state, which is that of the first subtle form whose seat is in the heart and which is the embryonic spiritual being. In this state the individual feels himself to be borne along like a wave on the primordial ocean, moving in unison with the universal vital principle which gives rise to the rhythm of the beating of his heart and the inhale and exhale of his breathing. This explains the power of rhythm which is the foundation of all rites of initiation designed to facilitate our return to the Principial Unity. Through these rites the individual attains to virtual immortality, i.e. the Paradise or salvation of Western religion. Moreover, conditions differ according to the spiritual world of which the dead person formed a part and into which he is integrated. Those for whom transmigration does not apply remain in Paradise to the end of the great universal cycle. This path of the dead and posthumous states in general implies a possible return to the world of manifestation. The Ancients symbolically placed this entrance to such states under the sign of Cancer and called the path the *Way of the Ancestors*, i.e. those who, representing previous cycles, are destined to become the seeds of the cycle of the future.

Beyond this sphere the luminous reign of the Ether begins, finishing in the sphere of Brahma, the realm of formlessness. The way to this state, which is destined for those who had experienced deliverance (*mukta*) through understanding, was placed under the sign of Capricorn and was called the *Way of the Gods*, who symbolize the various higher states the individual has to pass through on his heavenly ascent. This transformation is a passing beyond the world of forms for our bodies, through a 'resurrection body' and for our souls, in 'the light of glory'. The only positive criteria by which the individual can estimate his progress through the different stages of this way are visions of colours diffracted by the light of glory which give rise to the beatific vision. At first one only sees dazzling flashes, like lightning, which gradually become fixed in the colour appropriate to each stage, which corresponds also to a different angelic state. The different veils of light and darkness are gradually torn aside and each unveiling corresponds to the emergence of a faculty, the intelligence, the heart, the spirit, superconsciousness, the arcane. 'God', the Sufis say, 'is hidden by seventy thousand veils of light and shadow. If he were to be uncovered the brilliance of his face would reduce the universe to ashes.' That is why black light denotes union. The divine light enables us to see but its source remains hidden.

Beyond the three worlds of manifestation, the material, the subtle, and the formless, a further state of non-manifestation exists which is the Principal of the other three. It is the world of the *En-Soph*, of the Hebrew Kabbala, 'Deliverance' in the Hindu teaching, and the Supreme Identity of Islam. This non-manifest state is reached when one has passed beyond the manifest, beyond the darkness, when one can see as the Hindu texts say 'the other face of darkness'. It is the state of the Hindu *yogi* and of the Universal Man of Islam.

The Universal Man, principle of all states which virtually coexist, remains only a possibility, since full realization has not been given to Him. In Him all states are found, freed from whatever limited them, in absolute plenitude. Supreme understanding is in effect identical with the totality of reality and coextensive with Universal Possibility. This state is ineffable except by negative concepts, non-finite or infinite non-duality. From the viewpoint of the world of manifestation it is deliverance, from the side of Principle it is supreme identity. Deliverance, understanding, and identity are all that one and the same state in which the subject, the means and the object are one.

Only the *yogi*, who corresponds to the *pneumaticoi* of the Gnostics, can attain to such a deliverance whilst still alive here (*jivan-mukti*) whilst other individuals as we have seen can only aspire to entry into Paradise after their death. After crossing the Sea of the Passions and the Stream of Forms, the *yogi* reaches the Great Peace in his possession of the Self. For him separation, ignorance, and fear no longer have any meaning. He sees all, whilst remaining in Himself, United with Blessedness, 'fused but not confused', to use an expression of Eckhart. Shankara said that there was no degree of being above that of the *yogi* and he distinguishes in him three inseparable attributes: childlikeness (*balya*), wisdom (*panditya*), and *mauna*, the great solitude and silence. The childlike state is comparable to the Taoist concept of simplicity and the poverty of the Sufis.

The theory of cycles and so of stages teaches us that all ends are provisional. Although the theory is concerned with quite exceptional cases and refers to a cosmic function rather than to any realization, a word must be said about what René Guénon calls *realization by descent*.

With regard to this Guénon distinguishes two aspects or phases in the realization of the individual, the one being an ascending process, which we have described and which is in principle open to all capable of realizing it, and another which is very exceptional, a descent. The individual who is at rest in the non-manifest has completed his journey, the one who redescends fulfills a predestined role as messenger or avatar. This divine missionary is commissioned to bring his spiritual influence to the inhabitants of this mortal world. This is the role of all the great prophets in history, the founders of religions, the creators of rites; Hindu thought for example teaches that in this present cycle we have already seen ten avatars of Vishnu. When the essential means of understanding have been obscured to the point when they are quite unknown and human life has lost its *raison d'être*, an avatar comes to adapt the eternal revelation to the new situation of the world.

Each avatar in a cycle follows a procedure which is that of a manifestation of which he is the pole. The descending path becomes the manifestation and from this point of view initiation can be seen as the actualization in the individual of the same principle which in the cycle as a whole appears as the eternal avatar. The prophets and founders of religions are, from the divine viewpoint, victims, and their life has a sacrificial character. It is worth noting that the *Puranas* teach that the primordial avatar in the cycle in which we are is fire and must return at the end of the cycle to set the world on fire and reduce it to ashes. Heraclitus, the Stoics, the Apocalypse, and the Puranas all make fire the means of the world's renovation and of its final reintegration. If we wish to find a criterion by which to judge the completeness and so the perfection of an act, so difficult to discern in the human order, no better can be found than that of the eternal avatar, the ultimate symbol of harmony and balance.

PART TWO

THE HISTORICAL FORMS

At the beginning of the 20th century from the traditional point
of view one could still distinguish three great groups of civilizations: the Ancient, which had long disappeared and had not left
any qualified interpreters, the Western, which only retains the
vestiges of the great common medieval civilizations, and finally
the Eastern, whose social framework, no matter how degraded
it had become, still possessed a living tradition. This situation
was in sharp contrast to that of the Middle Ages when other civilizations, though remote, were nevertheless based on the same principles so that the elite from East and West could understand and
appreciate one another.

Today, when Western materialism and the reign of the machine
have conquered the earth, the contrast has dwindled to almost the
opposite. No differences any longer separate East and West and
traditional thought is universally condemned so its role has compelled it to return to obscurity and secrecy. Nevertheless, the
ancient traditional ways are taking their time to die and will never
completely disappear. The East today still has enough spiritual
masters for the picture that one can draw today to have more than
merely historical interest but also a certain immediacy.

So having in the first part of this book revealed the deep identity of the doctrine as it has been variously described, we will
endeavour in this second part to identify and contrast the various ways in which it has been put into practice. Whilst not being
unaware of the existence of various minor traditions in America
and Africa and in Siberia, we have nevertheless limited ourselves
to the esoteric aspects of the great religions of the world; Hinduism, Buddhism (both Tibetan and Japanese), Chinese Taoism, Judaism, Islam, and Christianity (both Orthodox and Catholic).
Esotericism is a relative term which refers to the inner aspects
of a religious teaching and to the deeper meaning of its external
social aspects, to which it is inseparably linked. We have, therefore, felt it necessary to sketch the principal features of each
religion (except Christianity) before showing their esoteric significance and how this is embodied in them or detached from
them.

I
THE EAST
1.
The Hindu Tradition

Hindu doctrine is founded on the *Vedas*, an extremely ancient collection of scriptures composed in Sanskrit verse by the *rishis*, legendary wise men who 'heard' them. For Hindus the Vedas are supernatural in origin, preceding the manifestation of the world, and are eternal by nature. This understanding is based on the primordial nature of sound as a cosmic function since audible vibration gave rise to the revelation, as it did to the world. These Hindu hymns and narratives relate the birth of the world in the form of theogonies, of battles between gods and titans, that is to say, between antagonistic forces which represent former and latter or higher and lower states of the cosmos. By this means the appearance of duality at the heart of the infinite and then the appearance of multiplicity are explained. Duality reveals itself to be a provisional equilibrium between opposing phenomena which are the metamorphoses of the One by assimilation or transformation. The Infinite is broken down, absorbed, and becomes nutriment. At each level this mutual absorption is conceived of as dilation and contraction, being born and dying. God creates man and destroys him. Man absorbs his God and then reveals him. God's sacrifice is creation; man's sacrifice is action. The fact of devouring and destroying is the only formally permanent reality. As there can be no sacrifice without an officiant and a victim, each one alternately makes the sacrifice and *is* the sacrifice. *Agni* and *Soma*, fire and holocaust. The worshippers of Vishnu give precedence to the preservative function of sacrifice and those of Shiva to its transforming function. But willingly or not, we all participate in a continual sacrifice, which is life itself. In the Vedas and hence in Hinduism this doctrine of sacrifice is central.

This increasing transformation of all things gives them an illusory nature which the Hindus call *Maya* and which indicates the phantasmagoria of nature, whose hidden energy is personified in the feminine aspect of each god, *Shakti*. So Maya becomes the symbol of a hidden reality. It is not error but misleading appearance, true but only partially and provisionally so. We are all dupes of Maya, which is the result of the inexhaustible metamorphoses of nature.

In the Vedas everything is related to the Supreme Principle. This Principle may be thought of as both personal and impersonal; as impersonal it is called *Brahma* and as personal *Ishwara*. Brahma is beyond all conceptual thought, but it is manifested by its energies, the shakti and their familiars, the innumerable gods of Hindu polytheism. In India they say that there are 333 million gods, an eminently symbolic number. Ideally for Hinduism each individual would have his own god, who is thus everywhere, for each individual's conception of god is incompatible with anyone else's. So there are innumerable gods, from the most naturalistic of idols to simple non-figurative designs, the geometric *yantras*. The divinity is revealed equally well in an animal, a flower, or a fruit as it is in the prayers, the *mantras*, each one of which evokes a special aspect of the divinity. The very multiplicity of these approaches, which makes polytheism possible, also gives a more exact and more striking idea of the mystery.

This apparent polytheism, however, does not prevent the more informed believer from rising above the multiplicity of gods to the one unity, or rather to non-duality; this latter word means not one or unique, but identical, or conveys the idea of 'all in all and like all'. In India esoteric thought appears in the full light of day in that there is an immaterial continuity between the outer and the inner, the visible and the hidden, the most everyday superstition and the highest metaphysic.

So although Hinduism has no official ecclesiastical structure or authority, something which is perhaps not altogether an advantage in an era as troubled as ours, nevertheless their tradition is strong enough to reject the most dangerous heresies, notably those coming from Hindu modernists. For if Hinduism appears tolerant in our eyes, it is so concerned with exactness that it has no need to be defended, and it is not concerned with the same key issues as we are. If Hinduism is not interested in proselytism or conversion it is because in their eyes every one of us should accept the tradition into which he was born, his *dharma*, and it would be impossible and even impious for any one to wish to reject it. Such a change would in any case be pointless since all aspects of the divine are legitimate and there are no 'false gods'.

Hinduism believes that in order to draw near to the Invisible Presence and escape from the illusion of Maya there is no better means than gnosis; understanding of the doctrine. Since action is no antidote to ignorance, only understanding gained by the study of the Vedas can dissipate it. The Vedas are divided into four sections of which the main one is the *Rig-Veda* composed of about a thousand ritual hymns. These are followed by prose passages for meditation called *brahamanas*, and some fragmentary notes on an esoteric teaching called *Upanishads* which express the quintessence of the Vedas and of Hindu wisdom. The Vedas eventually gave rise to six doctrinal formulations known as *darshanas* or points of view. Two among these darshanas are of special interest from the esoteric viewpoint; the *Vedanta* (or end of the Veda) and the *Yoga*. The Vedanta, which is based on the Upanishads, is in such concentrated form that it has been the object of commentaries by the greatest and wisest men of India, the most celebrated of these commentaries are those of Shankaracharya which are Shivaite in outlook, and that of Ramanuja which is Vishnuite.

The Upanishads and their commentaries teach, as far as it is possible in words, that the ultimate object of understanding is a personal realization which is inseparable from the theory which is its guide, it is a lived metaphysic. For Hinduism never separates the doctrine from the way in which it is applied. The sacred scriptures declare themselves to be useless without experience to which they are but a prelude. In order to achieve realization 'the preoccupations of the world, the enslavement of bodily needs, and even the scriptures themselves must all be rejected'. The principle of non-duality which dominates Hindu thought is clearly affirmed in the sacred texts. The Western concepts of monism and monotheism are only approximations to the concept of non-dualism. In order to convey the sense of disorientation, like a palace of mirages, which the concept of identity induced by the reading of the Upanishads produces, it is better to use the expression non-contradiction, that is to say, equivalence. The leit-motif of the doctrine being all is *Atman*, and the Atman which is spirit is the Self.

Yoga describes the means whereby union (*yoga*) and ecstasy (*samadhi*) may be achieved. The various kinds of yoga are differentiated by the degree of realization which they assist. There are four varieties and branches, each one of which stresses the use of a different element or faculty: the body, the mind, the psyche, or the intellect. Although differing, all are effective. The *yogi* acquires successively purity, vigour for life, mental peace, bodily lightness, and spiritual concentration. One of his most powerful tools is control of his breathing by the recitation of mantras, by which means the force in man corresponding to the cosmic power of Shakti, the Divine Mother, is awakened. Shakti in modern India has become the great goddess of Tantric and popular Hinduism. The achievement of this realization requires a *guru* in whom wisdom is incarnate. For as the scriptures say: 'A father may teach his son or a gifted disciple what is the immensity of the infinite, but no one else.'

In times when the tradition has become obscured, initiates will adopt the cult of Shiva. The relevant texts, the *Tantras*, reflect this in that they are a closely guarded secret and rarely published. The body of man is thought of as the cup of sacrifice. That store of bodily power which the uninitiated waste so prodigally is used by the yogi to be transmuted into spiritual power, which he absorbs into himself, letting it fall again on him like a refreshing dew, giving him a new birth and mastery of his acts and desires. He attains *samadhi* and becomes a *jivan-mukta*, one who has found deliverance in his lifetime. 'All nature has become his I. He sees the spirit which infuses everything. He can commune with the Self within himself.'

2.

Buddhism

The Buddha, son of the prince of a country near Nepal, founder of a religious order in his lifetime, has after his death become the god of a universal religion. He did not bring to India an entirely new teaching but a way of life based on an irrefutable truth, the Law of *Dharma*. Its starting point is the existence of evil and suffering. 'I only teach one thing, the origin and the end of evil', he said. In order to overcome suffering he traced its origin to action, which is born of desire and is in its turn the result of ignorance.

This is what led the Blessed One to enunciate his four truths: suffering is universal, ignorance of the dharma as the cause of suffering, the obligation to end suffering, and so the removal of ignorance in all its manifestations: indifference, unawareness, and sloth. For ignorance presupposes that we are the dupes of the multiplicity of things which are by nature so conflicting and contradictory. Buddha was delivered from suffering by transcending appearance and if it is possible for us after him also to transcend them, it is because these appearances are 'empty' and it is the recognition of this emptiness that leads to *nirvana*.

For Buddhism nothing is permanent. 'Nothing in this world can be regarded as the Self (or Spirit)', he has said. Everything consists of temporary conglomerations. Even the individual self has no essential reality, it is only the temporary meeting place of changing influences. The individual is in a constant state of decay and renewal. And if, as Hinduism teaches, there is transmigration, one cannot assume that there is any constant entity that transmigrates; transmigration is an act without an agent or an object, just as there is the appearance of an individual self but not the reality of it. To make things clearer one could say that when an individual dies the Self which is eternal transmigrates, that is to say, the universal Self continues to give life to other contingent beings.

Deliverance therefore is not for the individual self, but for the universal Self which can never become an individual self. We can enjoy this deliverance when we are no longer our separate selves but have become one with the Supreme Identity.

This feeling of the impermanence of the self brings with it suffering, through which, however, deliverance can come provided that we gain enlightenment, on which Buddhism formally places the greatest emphasis. On this Buddha is as strict as Brahmanism, perhaps even more so, since he places such emphasis on it that the method of attaining it becomes an esoteric rite. A conscience always on the alert and an unfailing intellectual insight must control all our acts; not that the Master recommends great asceticism, but on the contrary, he recommends a middle way based on contemplation. 'One becomes a Brahman by one's deeds', he says. All beings are the heirs of their deeds.

It is natural that a cosmic loving kindness should be the supreme Buddhist virtue, universal compassion. Authentic Buddhists are outstanding by their total detachment from life and by a profound pity for humanity, driven onwards by the desire for life and the illusion of happiness. 'That all things may enjoy felicity' is one of the exemplary maxims of Buddhism. In this it is an heir to Brahmanism, as is shown by the sublime epilogue to the *Mahabharata* when the hero Yudhisthira refuses to enter Paradise unless his dog can come with him.

Buddha was not at all concerned about the caste system and he was never worried by the social implications of his actions, hence the progressive decline of Buddhism in India. It was quite natural that the Buddhist preaching should lead to the foundation of an order of monks vowed to contemplation. But just because of this Buddhism was able to expand and receive a remarkable welcome. The Vedic doctrine at this point of social structure was identified with the national spirit so much that the notion of a man not of Hindu blood being converted to Hinduism was unthinkable, and even repulsed with horror. Buddhism, on the other hand, proved to be an admirable vehicle for the expansion of Indian spirituality. Buddhist missionaries spread to China, Japan, Tibet, Burma, and Thailand.

The objective of Buddhist monks is the achievement of the awakening of *nirvana*, but as it would be presumptuous to claim to have achieved this straight away, their rule urged them to follow the path towards becoming like Buddha by becoming a *bodhisattva*, i.e. possessing the qualities of Buddha before his enlightenment.

Buddhist enlightenment is composed of many stages, both formal and informal. We will limit ourselves to describing the eightfold path which consists of right beliefs, right thought, right speech, right conduct, right vocation, right effort, right meditation, right concentration. The Buddha himself only showed people the way, leaving to each individual the responsibility of following it, for as he declared, 'No one can help you but yourself'. The objective is a gnosis or knowledge which is incommunicable. The Buddha is a *yogi* or an awakened one, which is the true meaning of the word Buddha. He remained faithful to the spirit of Hinduism as when he declared: 'Possess the Self (the Spirit) as lamp and refuge . . . nothing is more precious to him who attains it than the Self'. In Buddhism the idea of God is replaced by that of the Law, the two are fundamentally one. For this Law is the Principle. 'He who looks at me looks at the Law', he said.

The essentially esoteric nature of Buddhism has enabled it to adapt to various non-Indian exoteric forms, notably in Tibet where in alliance with the ancient Tibetan religion Bon-Po (or Red Bonnets), it gave rise to lamaistic Buddhism. Although this path is as difficult as all the others, it is considered especially suitable for our time. Before the Chinese invasion of Tibet, the monks who followed this path lived in hermitages protected by all sorts of solitude, from that of a cell to that of an isolated hut amongst the high peaks of Tibet. Tantric rites resemble closely those of the yogi but the prayers are Buddhist. As the Buddha never wished to deny the Principle but at the same time not to give it a name, it has been possible for his teaching to be called a non-doctrine. It has been expressed by the impermanence of every point of view. Every individual at any given moment represents only one state of being. From the material point of view he is matter, from the viewpoint of energy he is energy, from the point of view of mind he is intelligence, from the point of view of transience he is transient. Buddhism is the way of 'empty forms' and its consummation is *nirvana*, the abolition of all limitations.

3.

Chinese Taoism

The Far Eastern tradition in its most ancient form is deemed to have originated with the legendary first Chinese Emperor, Fo-Hi, whose name denotes an intellectual function rather than an individual. He is said to have written three works of which only one has come down to us, the I Ching or *Book of Change*, which makes use of very simple graphic symbols consisting of unbroken and broken lines. It is said that in order to preserve in writing the teaching on the Primordial Tradition which he had received, Fo-Hi lifted up his eyes to heaven and then lowered them to the earth and wrote on his tablets the eight *Kua*, the fundamental symbols in the Chinese tradition. Each Kua, or trigram, is constructed of three lines, which are either continuous or broken, thus giving eight different combinations. The unbroken line represents *yang*, the positive pole and expansive power of manifestation, the broken line represents *yin*, the negative pole and contracting force of manifestation. These two poles yin and yang dominate all the classifications of Chinese science and are the elements of the primary duality which unite to form (or derive from) the Principial (metaphysical) Unity and which the Chinese call the *Tao*, that is to say, the way or principle. There are two Kua which are especially noteworthy; the one which consists of three unbroken lines, which symbolizes Active Perfection, and the one of three broken lines, which symbolizes Perfection in its Passive form. Two Kua superimposed form a six-line figure or hexagram. As there are 64 different combinations which can form these hexagrams, 64 hexagrams compose the simplest and completest metaphysical alphabet and it is one which Fo-Hi used to compose the I-Ching. It is so universal in character that it has been interpreted in many different ways which are not mutually exclusive; astronomical, social, metaphysical, predictive, and so on. But the abstract nature of the hexagrams renders the book virtually untranslatable and some form of initiation is necessary in order to understand it correctly. As a later Taoist writer said: 'Ten will read, one will understand, ten thousand will not.'

So let us move forward to the sixth century BC to find a more accessible rendering of Taoist wisdom. It was at this period that the two complementary aspects of Chinese tradition, the exoteric and the esoteric, Confucianism and Taoism, were settled in a fashion that endured for many centuries. The Confucian aspect was concerned with external social relationships and the Taoist with the interior personal aspect. The great teacher of Taoism was Lao Tzu who was archivist at the imperial court of the Chou dynasty. He left only one work, the *Tao Te Ching*, but the *Kuan Yin Tzu* or 'Book of Concordant Actions and Reactions' by his disciple Chuan Tzu contains much of his teaching. It is said to be influenced by Mahayana Buddhism.

The Tao is the Chinese name for the Principle. 'There is one thing that is invariably complete. Before Heaven and Earth were, it is already there', says the author of the Tao, and he begins his work by saying: 'The Tao that can be expressed is not the eternal Tao. The name that can be named is not the eternal name. Non-existence I call the beginning of Heaven and Earth; Existence I call the mother of individual beings'; and later he writes: 'One looks and sees nothing for the Way is absence. One listens and hears nothing for the Way is silence. One touches and feels nothing for the Way is emptiness.' It is for this reason that it is said that whoever asks questions about the Tao and whoever gives answers are both equally ignorant.

However, all that exists in the cosmos stems from the Principle. 'The Tao created one, he created two, and he created the ten thousand things.' The first cause acts so naturally that no one realizes its action. 'The Tao works by doing nothing and if it seems never to do anything, it is because it is acting unceasingly.' So one does not notice movement which is uniform, permanent, and continuous, which conforms to the very law of our existence, any more than one is aware of the changes in our physiological state or of the rotation of the earth. Thus it is that the Tao is both the means and the end, to follow Tao is to be identical with it.

This formless principle acts through the opposing energies yang and yin whose harmonious balance is that of the Principle itself. This notion implies that every breach of this balance jeopardizes the world order since every action is necessarily followed by an equal and opposite reaction, as is taught by the *Kuan Yin Tzu*.

From this understanding arises the principle of 'least or non-action': 'Action and reaction follow man like his shadow.' If on the practical level the reaction sometimes appears to be a reward or a punishment, for the Taoist this moral interpretation is irrelevant. Taoism in accordance with this belief recommends that the wise man remain still at the centre of the wheel of existence. 'To see all in the primordial undifferentiated unity, this is true understanding', said Chang Tzu, the greatest thinker and prose writer of ancient China. The most obvious sign of a mind superior to both heaven and earth is its imperturbable serenity. The sage should apply the golden rule of non-action in all circumstances, in human government for example. 'Ruling a country is like cooking small fish', says Lao Tzu, that is to say, rule so very gently that people are unaware that they are being ruled.

As with all other initiations the Taoist path aims at union with the Principle. Its method is just as arduous as any other but it is not well adapted to any one other than the Chinese. It has even been said that Lao Tzu only confided his teaching to two disciples, who themselves did not share it with more than ten others. In Taoism, patience is the greatest of the virtues. Lieh Tzu, one of the greatest Taoist teachers, said that it was only after five years that his master smiled at him for the first time and only after ten years did he permit him to sit on his mat. The Taoist method consists of enhancing the yang and eliminating the yin and resembles closely the methods of Hindu yoga, but it uses the symbolism of alchemy. The body becomes the 'little crucible', the fire for which is fed by the absorption of air and light, a process known as 'the bath of the heart'. This reintegration is assisted by the preparation of *aurum potabile* (drinkable gold) which can be done by means of Chinese alchemy. Parallel with this incantatory ritual to nourish with yang, the 'pearl' or 'embryo of immortality' which comes into being in the cavern of the heart and which the initiate lifts by patient exercises up to the top of his head, where this subtle form is set free. This departure is accompanied by a feeling of ecstacy in which all physical sensations disappear by 'dissolution' and where the soul is concentrated by coagulation (the *solve et coagula* of alchemical theory). At this moment the soul leaves its earthly envelope and ascends to the world above. This absence of the soul from the body may appear to last a long time but in fact does not generally last more than a few seconds.

Union with the Principle dispels all the dissonant elements in the initiate and establishes perfect harmony between him and the world. He has lost his own individuality, his initiative, and his name. He has achieved the primordial simplicity, and by the integration of the vital principles, he reaches a state of silent union with the universe and true peace of heart. He knows all, without knowing how he knows. He has become a 'Transcendent Man'.

4.

Zen Buddhism

When in AD 520 the twenty-eighth Buddhist patriarch Bodhid-harma visited China to preach the doctrines of the Enlightened One, he taught them canonical meditation which is truly *contemplatio* (in Sanskrit: *dhyana*). The word *dhyana* was transcribed by the Chinese as *tchanna* or *tch'an*, which in Japanese became *zenna* or *zen*. In China itself two hundred years were sufficient for Taoism and Buddhism to achieve a true symbiosis under the spiritual leadership of Hui Neng Ta Ching, the sixth Chinese patriarch and the father of tch'an Buddhism which was to experience a wonderful flowering in the 9th century under the aristocratic T'ang dynasty in South China.

In 552 Buddhism was introduced from Korea into Japan, but it was not until 1191 that the Japanese monk Eisai returned from China bringing with him the tch'an system which was to take its most original form in Japan under the name of Zen. Buddhism has three disciplines for the achievement of self-realization, the ritual invocation of the name of Buddha (*nembutsu*), intellectual meditation (*ko-an*), and intuitive contemplation. Zen, without abandoning the first two, as we know adopted the third; the Zen masters tell us that Zen cannot be explained.

There is a famous scene in the life of Buddha in which he presented a lotus-flower to the monks of his congregation. This gesture was only understood by his favourite disciple Mahakasyapa who responded with a smile, which was the sign of illumination, that most secret experience.

Zen teaching tells us that in its original perfection the mind of man perceived reality directly. What prevents him from seeing it so are the words he uses to describe his experience, which is distorted when he tries to explain it. In Zen our worst enemies are words and discursive reasoning which obscure our intuitive understanding, which otherwise is objective, exhilarating, direct, and instantaneous. Understanding can only be achieved by living it. By this way of spiritual liberation, comprehension of the self is made more precise and more profound, to such an extent that it reveals to us 'our original face which we had before we were born'.

Zen explains nothing; it shows us the living truth as the Buddha showed his lotus to the monks. It brings about a direct apprehension, above intellectual understanding which comes later. This is what gives it its most unexpected and most revealing character. One lives life before understanding it and the will is antecedent to logic. The answer to a question does not throw light on the thing in question because the answer is determined not by the thing itself but by the question about it. The true answer is not found in words but in contemplating the object in such a way that we experience a state of ecstacy which the Japanese call *satori*. In the course of satori the Noble Wisdom shows itself in us. At the level of exoteric religion there is no absolute criterion of sincerity or authenticity. The use of the language of the dominant orthodoxy can convince no one, whereas on the level of experience no verbal illusion is possible. The adept cannot lie to himself or others. The nature of his satori makes it self-authenticating. It is the measure of zen and its *raison d'etre*. We should not forget that zen is an offshoot of Buddhism, that is to say, teaching which denies the permanence of the self, as is implied in the famous dialogue between the Bodhidharma and his disciple Houei-ko. 'I can't manage to pacify my spirit', said Houei-ko. 'Show me your spirit so that I can pacify it', said the master. 'But that's just it. I can't find it.' 'Then your request has been granted', replied Bodhidharma. The same point is made more succinctly in this brief exchange: 'What is my self?' 'What would you do with a self?'

As it comprises no dialectic or didactic formulation Zen can only be learnt from a master. A long period of study, sometimes called 'the long maturing of the sacred matrix', has to be gone through, and the seeker has to live in harmony with this inner self-realization. No matter whether this life is lived in mountain retreat or in the busy rush of a city, it should combine extreme simplicity, absolute independence, no idleness, and strict secrecy. Poverty, emptiness, moral nakedness, purity, and sometimes deliberate commonplaceness, such are the characteristics of a system in which the self is tested and refined until it is virtually transparent. Generally this period of training is spent in a monastery which has a meditation hall where the practical exercises are performed. For, whereas in India the monks beg for their livelihood, in China and Japan they work for it. St Paul was not the first to say he who does not work does not eat. The meditation hall or *zendo* is absolutely bare and in it the monks eat, sleep, and work. There they engage in zen's most original activity, I mean the ko-an.

This consists of a question or a short phrase, an anecdote or a theme composed by the master or chosen by him from the 1700 ko-an worked out in past times. The disciple must use it to stabilize all his mental processes and call a halt to all his discursive reasoning. In order to do this the ko-an must be either absurd or insoluble. There are many famous ko-an such as: 'All things return to the One, but where does the One return to?' and 'What is the last and final word of truth?' or 'Who is Buddha?' and its opposite, 'Who is not Buddha?' These phrases, the absurd or paradoxical answers made by the masters, mimicking them in a kind of answer; silences, the yes-yes and no-no, and even blows with a stick, are all used to awaken the student and to prove that spiritual experience takes precedence over speech and that Zen is the product of living and that satori springs from the depths of one's own being. For one cannot pass judgement on life since it is both what is being judged and what judges it (the Hindu maya); thus it is the best symbol for metaphysical truth, as is suggested by the famous fable of the three vinegar tasters. It is said that Confucius, Buddha, and Lao Tzu met in front of a jar of vinegar (the symbol of life). Each one dipped his finger in to taste it. Confucius found it acid, Buddha thought it bitter, and Lao Tzu thought it sweet.

The form of Zen adopted by the aristocratic Samurai in the 13th century moulded the Japanese character. Everywhere one can discern its spirit of elegant purity, both in the suggestive simplicity of their watercolours, in the subtle brevity of Hai Ku poems, in the art of archery and in their garden design, but above all in the tea ceremony. In all things those faithful to Zen teachings endeavour to reproduce life in all its spontaneity and continual improvisation, without recourse to possible rationalizations. The tea ceremony, which some believe originated with Lao Tzu himself, has become an outstanding feature of Japanese civilization. The tea-house (*sukiya*), small and of a refined poverty, ought to unite in itself nature and artifice, purity and elegance, modesty and perfection. There is a very popular tale by Riku, the celebrated tea-master. Riku had given his son the job of cleaning up the garden through which his friends were to pass. Over and over again the young man had washed the steps and the stone lanterns, had watered the mosses and lichens and had removed the leaves and the weeds from the path. The master was never satisfied and said impatiently, 'You young fool, this is not how to clean a garden.' Dashing forward he ran and shook a tree in order to spread its gold and purple leaves on the ground; showing that man-made purity and beauty must know how to be concealed by nature.

5.

The Hebrew Tradition

Islam occupies a very important place in the Far East, but like Judaism and Christianity, it is one of the three Abrahamic religions; so we should begin with the most ancient of these, Judaism.

The esoteric tradition of the Jews is called the Kabbala, a word which simply means tradition. The Kabbala is the oral revelation which Moses received at the same time as he received the Tables of the Law, and it explains the deeper meaning of the Torah. Since the Kabbala is based on the letters of the Hebrew alphabet, to which are also attributed numerical values, it is a Jewish esoteric system, and even if one is a Christian, it cannot be validly applied to any other language. No other tradition is more exclusive and none more secret. Kabbalists have always been few in number and not particularly anxious to share their knowledge. It is not that there are not plenty of manuscript sources, they are abundant, but they remain largely unpublished. The best known are the *Sefer Yetsirah* (or Book of Creation), the *Sefer Ha-Zohar* (or Book of Divine Splendour). The *Zohar* which was written in a late form of Aramaic mixed with Hebrew and a number of deformed foreign words, purports to be a free commentary on the Pentateuch; the section on Genesis occupies a good half of the whole. This esoteric commentary uses three means of interpretation, *Gematria, Notarikon*, and *Temurah*. Gematria uses the numerical values of the letters for various forms of calculation, including the search for other words of equal value. Notarikon uses the interpretation of the letters in a word as a new word or as an abbreviation of a whole sentence. Temurah uses the two other methods to interchange other letters according to certain prescribed laws. In addition to the commentary, the *Zohar* contains eighteen short theosophical treatises which make references to the celebrated second century Rabbi Semeon ben Yohai, whose

teachings are reported in these writings. The objective of the Kabbalists is identical with that of initiates in all other traditions;
the return to God. Since this return has to follow in the reverse
direction the process of Creation, it is easy to understand why
so much attention is paid to the book of Genesis, which occupies
a central position in these meditations. Creation is understood
as the outworking of the Divine Energies as expressed by the Word.
Creation is born out of nothingness, or rather out of the void (*Tohu-
Bohu*), an incomprehensible nothingness since here we are in the
realm of non-manifestation. It is the Divine Word which imposes
order on creation. In the process of manifestation Creation and
understanding are mutual and equivalent. The Divine Thought
is manifest as God or *Elohim* from whom emanates the Voice
or Word which, as the *Sefer Yetsirah* says, causes light to shine
from the primordial centre. The universe expands in the six directions of space (left, right, up, down, backwards, and forwards) from
the central point hidden in the mystery of the Interior Palace. This
point is the centre of space and time. Like the Talmud, the *Zohar*
divides the history of the world into six thousand-year periods,
prefigured by the six days of creation. The seventh day is the Sabbath and the seventh era that of the return to the Principle.

To explain the various steps to knowledge and the different stages
on the way to the restitution of the Primordial State, the Kabbala
uses a complex collection of symbols based on the Letters of the
Divine Name, of which the *Sefiroth* (the ten elementary and primordial numbers), sometimes called Palaces, are aspects. The Glory
of God is represented by a throne (Ezekiel 10: 1) which is hidden by the cosmic veil and by our human activities (cf., Hindu
maya). To reach this Throne one must pass through the Seven
Palaces, or rather the seven halls of the Holy Palace, these halls
each representing one of the seven degrees of perfection. This
Holy Palace is symbolic of the world's centre and according to
the *Sefer Yetsirah*, the place of manifestation of the *shekinah* or
divine radiance (identical with the *ruah ha-hodesh*, the Holy Spirit).
The Sefiroth or divine attributes are all subsumed in the shekinah.

Moses de Leon says that the Holy One can only be compre-
hended in His attributes by means of which He created the world.
The mystery of 'the point of origin' is hidden in the impalpable
ether in which the original concentration takes place. The light
which illuminates the whole extended universe emanates from
this point (a point geometrically has location but no magnitude
and metaphysically neither location nor magnitude). The light
(Hebrew *aor*) springs from the etheric (*avir*) mystery. This hid-

den point is represented by the Hebrew letter I (*Yod*) which symbolizes the Principle; from it all the other letters are formed. When the Yod was given a form, all that remained of the mystery was hidden in light. This is an excellent example of Kabbalistic thought since it can be put in the form of an equation: avir - i = aor.

The Kabbala distinguishes four worlds dominated by the *En-Sof* or Infinite, between it and our earthly cosmos. 1. *Atsiluth*, the world of Emanation. 2. *Beriah*, the world of Creation. 3. *Yetsirah*, the world of Formation. 4. *Atsiyah*, the world of making or action. The *Sefer Yetsirah* explains the creation of the world by postulating thirty-two paths, the 10 sefiroth and the 22 letters of the Hebrew alphabet. These 22 letters also correspond to the 22 possible links which can be established between the 10 sefiroth. These sefiroth, whose name recalls the ten original numbers, also represent the Divine Names and also the Divine activities and the Divine attributes, which delineate the spheres in which they operate. The *Zohar* calls them 'the depths of the Intellect'. They are in fact the principal determinations and the eternal causes of all creation. They correspond to the Divine Names of Islam and the uncreated powers of Orthodoxy.

Traditionally a tree is used to delineate the relationships between the sefiroth. The tree has three stems or trunks like columns, 'carved from the impalpable ether'. This tree is frequently shown reversed, its roots drawing their nourishment from the heavens and distributing it through the branches which touch the earth, like a celestial dew. The right hand column is that of Mercy and Grace, the lefthand that of Severity and Justice. The central column is the column of balance and unites the four principal sefiroth: the Crown, Harmony or Beauty, the Foundation, and the Kingdom. This central column can be related to the Tree of Life in the Garden of Eden, the world axis around which the cosmos turns. The correspondence of microcosm and macrocosm means that it is allowable to discern a correspondence between each *sefira* and a part of the body of Adam Kadmon, and consequently with our own bodies.

Adhesion to God (to use Gershom Scholem's expression, Hebrew *devekuth*) is the supreme aim of the Kabbalists. It requires a method of work which moves through the vision in the mirror, the exterior and inner countenance, intuition, love, and finally ecstatic union. It is by no means rare to find that when one comes to the exact description of method one encounters remarks such as, 'What remains to be said must not be imparted to everyone', the 'remains' being the technical rules governing the rites preparatory to ecstatic union.

When prayer constitutes the fundamental element in the method it is called 'The Way of Names', as Abulafia named it. To transcend thought Abulafia combined letters one with another in a deliberately arbitrary manner until he succeeded in banishing all discursive thought. He relates that for a whole night he succeeded in combining the seventy-two divine names in this way until he had completely transcended all mental activity.

This progress towards the Divine Throne was prepared for by long years of meditation and study, followed by fasts of between 12 and 40 days. The prayers were said in a bodily position corresponding to the shape of one of the Hebrew letters, and correct breathing was of the greatest importance. The soul could thus claim to pass through the Seven Palaces or Seven Heavens of tradition. At each stage a seal or bond was broken until the initiate reached the seventh stage, that of Adam Kadmon, the presence of the Light of Glory.

In conclusion, let us add that Hebrew has wrongly been considered to be the Sacred Language of the Christian Tradition, nevertheless Kabbalism has always played a part in Christian esoteric thought, as is confirmed by the existence of Kabbalists among the Greek Fathers.

6.

The Islamic Tradition

Islam, the third branch, growing as it were out of season from the Abrahamic stock, is the last important revelation given to our world, and it claims to surpass the two ancient monotheistic religions, Judaism and Christianity, in affirming this monotheism with unremitting severity. For the Muslim, God is the continuous creator, without intermediaries or secondary causes, whose Names are only to be called His attributes from the point of view of manifestation. The doctrine of Islam is above all that of Unity (*tawhid*) and of transcendence. As the Sura or Chapter in the Q'uran declares: 'He, Allah is One, he neither begets nor is begotten. He is without equal.' Because it puts great emphasis on the unity of the Principle, Islam is outstandingly esoteric in character. It does not, as do the gospels and the Jewish Torah, only tell man what he ought to do, but it also tells him what he is. And if Judaism is a Way of action and Christianity is a Way of active love, Islam is a Way of knowledge and balance, whose unwavering certainty on the practical level seems to be intolerant. The Witnessing (*shahadah*) to this certainty is expressed in the formula: 'There is no God but God', the saying of which is enough to make one a Muslim. So it might be said that there is in fact a sense in which we are all natural Muslims, i.e. those who submit to the Universal Law, to the Divine Will, whether we recognize it or not, and that this first announcement of Witnessing is a simple statement of fact. It points out our dependence and consequently also a transcendence which every clearsighted man is bound to acknowledge.

The second part of the Shahadah, 'And Mohammad is his prophet', affirms the mission of Mohammad as God's messenger and accepts the revelation of the Q'uran. As in Judaism the Islamic revelation is bound to the symbolism of 'the book'. The universe is a book in which the letters are the different elements of the cosmos. According to the Q'uran, and above all according to the *hadith* or sacred traditions, the Prophet ordained five pillars of support for Islam: the witnessing, the annual fast of Ramadan, canonical prayers to be recited five times daily, the yearly tithing, and the pilgrimage to Mecca to be performed at least once in a lifetime. The deeper significance of these ordinances becomes clear if one pushes them to their limits. Prolonged fasting results in death to the world, prolonged prayer will lead to sanctification, tithing repeated until one's resources are exhausted leads to spiritual poverty, pilgrimage as a permanent state of mind leads to union.

Of the five pillars of Islam, prayer is the most continuously performed of religious rites; as a Muslim mystic has said: 'Prayer is a river flowing past my door in which I wash myself five times a day.' It must be governed by the heart, and this necesssary intention is symbolized by the orientation towards Mecca (*gibleh*) without which the prayer is not valid. The initial invocation in all prayer consists of the first words of the Q'uran, the *Fatiha* (or opening): 'In the Name of God the all-Merciful, the all-Compassionate.'

It is said that the Fatiha contains in essence the whole of the Q'uran, and that the invocation above contains the whole of the Fatiha, and that the invocation itself is contained in the letter 'ba', which is the first letter of the first word of the invocation, *Bis-milla*. The letter 'ba' is in essence to be found in the diacritical dot which denotes it in the Arabic script. This thought has led certain mystics to compare the state of Union with the Divine to this single point.

As is the case in all the religions developing from the Abrahamic stock, Islam makes a very strong distinction between the high road of religion governed by the *sharia*, the exoteric aspect in fact, and inner truth *haqiqah*, known to initiates and deemed esoteric. The shariah is therefore a comprehensive guide to action. The haqiqah is pure understanding, the approach to which is facilitated by various paths (*tariqah*) or initiatic fraternities. The shariah is supported by faith whose centre is the heart, and by submission (*islam*) which embraces all aspects of being. Haqiqah is increased by means of the power in the metaphysical way (*tariqah*), the esoteric path to inner understanding.

This esotericism in Islam is not a recent addition, as some have suggested, but derives directly from the teaching of the Prophet, and every authentic tariqah is the heir to a succession or link (*selseleh* uniting it to him. Mohammad himself used to retire for meditation to a cave on mount Hira in the month of Ramadan during the years which preceded the first Q'uranic revelation. He continued this practice later on in the mosque at Medina. There are in theory sixty-four authentic fraternities (*tourouq*, pl. of tariqah) whose members are known as *mourid* (disciple) or *faquir* (poor). The spiritual masters of such groups who by virtue of their lives and fame are deemed to be saintly, receive the name of *sufi* (pure). The first Sufis formed fraternities at Basra and Kufah in the eighth and ninth centuries AD. Among them we should single out Rabia al-Adawiyya, the great female mystic, and Hasan al Basri. In the middle of the ninth century al-Junaid wrote a comprehensive treatise on Sufism. In Persia with Yazid al Bistami, the legendary hero of Persian Sufism, Sufi spirituality made use of poetic symbolism. The chief exponent of mystical poetry of this sort is Jalal al-Din Rumi. The greatest master of Arabic esoteric thought is Mohyid-din ibn Arabi who taught the most elevated metaphysical truths in his works *The Revelations of Mecca* and *The Gems of Wisdom*. In this flowering of Islamic mysticism one must not forget the important part played by Iranian *shi'ism*, the second main branch of Islam, after the *sunni*, whose followers were partisans of Ali as the Prophet's successor (and whose cousin and son-in-law he was). This spiritual stream separated in the eighth century into two branches, *imamism* and *Ismaelism*. Shi'ism produced its own notable Sufis, such as Semnani in the fourteenth century, and Amoli, who doctrinally was a disciple of the Sunni Ibn Arabi.

The surface simplicity of the doctrines of the Q'uran facilitates its interpretation at a much deeper level. In addition, so that one knows how to interpret them correctly, one must be linked to an authentic line of succession (selseleh) and to a master whose blessing one has received. Preliminary study of the doctrine results in one's being able to go beyond it by intuition of a higher order and with the assistance gained by practising those virtues which the Sufis identify with the different degrees of spirituality. The hierarchy of these virtues is one of the most valuable and obvious aspects of their realization summed up, as they all are, in spiritual poverty, sincerity, and true detachment, without which the others cannot exist. The different degrees of perfection are classified as either transitional states (*hal*) or definite stages (*maqam*). All these methods are gathered up under the aegis of the *dhikr* or recollection of God. The means of achieving recollection is the invocation of the Divine Name, remembering the famous

injunction to 'Worship God as if you saw Him, for if you do not
see Him, He sees you'. Recitation of the Q'uran, repetition of the
litany of the 99 Names of God, prepared for by fasting and retreat,
are powerful methods of approach. One of the most original
methods is the spiritual concert or sacred dance (*sama'*) as practised by the *darwish*. For although poetry and music are frowned
on by the *shariah*, they are nevertheless used by Sufis, especially
those groups in Iran.

The reward for the esoteric vocation is the achievement of the
Great Peace (*es-Sakinah*), which is in other terms the Divine
Presence at the centre of one's being and one of the most unmistak-
able criteria of Union. But because, in accordance with Sufi spirituality, the Divine Essence only reveals itself to the seeker as personal
revelation, he only sees himself in the Divine mirror. The invisible Essence is always beyond the mirror and beyond all dualism,
which we can never escape on earth. This is why the Sage advises
the seeker never to despair and not to pursue the unattainable;
paying more attention to the means rather than keeping his eye
always on the end. 'Do not weary your soul by always seeking
a higher state.'

The Great Peace is denoted by simplicity, a childlike state, being
without possessions, a stage on the pathway to Union, and the
ultimate extinction of the self. This detachment has led certain
mystics to despise the world and this sometimes takes the form
of non-conformity and humour. In the school of Hamdun al Qas-
sar, the *Malamatiyah*, this viewpoint is systematically expounded.
Forgetfulness of self leads one to take nothing seriously. This attitude when demonstrated in the world and vis-a-vis the shariah
has its dangers. Thinking in paradoxes can lead to martyrdom,
as we see in the case of al-Hallaj who said of God: 'To claim to
know him is ignorance, to persist in serving him is disrespectful,
to forbid yourself to struggle with him is folly, to allow yourself
to be misled by his peace is stupid, to discourse on his attributes
is to lose the way.' To concentrate on human contradictions which
still fail to express Divine Unity can lead to less talented disciples losing their way and ending up as atheists. Much more, the
abandonment of self can lead the God-intoxicated man, in affirming his identity with God, to say: 'I am the Truth (*ana al-Haqq*)',
a blasphemy which led al-Hallaj to torture and execution. In any
event the danger is that of an idolatry which mistakes the appearance for the essence, the journey for its end, a partial truth for
an absolute, a provisional stage for the final goal. We can understand how Bistami could have dared to say: 'Those most sepa-

rated from God are the ascetics by their ascesis, the devout by their devotion, the learned by their learning', only when we grasp that the ascetics and devout and learned were only so in appearance, since knowledge is only a tool which can be used well or badly, that asceticism is likewise a means and has no virtue in itself, and that devotion if it is an end in itself is a path that leads nowhere. The most splendid expression of Oneness was given in a poetic form by the great Mohyid din ibn Arabi when he said: 'My heart is capable of embracing all forms. It is the cloister of the Christian, the temple of the idols, the meadow of the gazelles, the Ka'aba of the pilgrim, the Tables of the Law of Moses, the Q'uran of the faithful. Love is my credo and my faith.'

II
THE WEST

7.

Esoteric Christianity

There is no need for us to give a detailed account of Christian
doctrine by which the West has lived for nearly two thousand
years. We will only try to give a sketch of the principal aspects
of Christian esotericism without touching on its spontaneous
manifestations in mysticism and poetry. We will limit ourselves
to studying the principal initiatic bodies of whose existence only
indirect proofs remain but which we are able to reveal thanks
to exceptional circumstances.

Since the authenticity of the links in the chain which unites
a tradition to its source is of decisive importance, it is necessary to return to that source in spite of the obscurity, no doubt
intended, by which it remains surrounded. The evidence of Flavius
Josephus enables us to distinguish three groups of believers who
were active during the life of Jesus, the Sadducees, a sacerdotal
group who interpreted the Pentateuch literally, the Pharisees,
adherents of a popular oral tradition, and finally the Essenes,
gathered together in a highly spiritual Pythagorean-type community. For a long time Jesus was suspected of being familiar with
this Essenian elite. The discovery at Qumran of six hundred
manuscripts containing their writings dating from the first century makes this a near certainty. Thanks to these manuscripts we
learn that the Essenes belonged to a very secret brotherhood. They
were known to each other as Sons of Light and called their doctrine The New Covenant. They lived a coenobitic life on the shores
of the Dead Sea in a monastery, traces of which have been discovered. The community consisted of three types of member:
postulants, novices, and initiates, for the last of whom was reserved
the revelation of a gnosis when they had completed three preparatory years. The principal rite was that of a sacred meal preceded
by rites of purification. Women were not admitted, they did not

use money, and they took an oath of secrecy. Their Superior, a member of the tribe of Levi and of the Aaronic priestly caste, was called 'The Master of Justice'. It is believed that one of them was condemned and executed by the order of the Sanhedrin. It is easy to see the parallels between these figures and these rites and those of infant Christianity. The marked silence of the Essenes at the coming of Christ leads one to believe that Jesus may have recruited his earliest disciples from amongst their ranks.

However, Christ's teaching went far behind the framework of Judaic ritual, which he himself respected and within which the Essenes wished to stay. Jesus emphasized the spiritual meaning of the Scriptures, as many of the Gospel sayings demonstrate. 'Whoso readeth let him understand . . .' 'He that hath ears to hear let him hear . . .' '. . . the mystery which from the beginning of the world was hid in God.' The limitations of the existing social order were clearly indicated in Jesus' saying: 'Render unto Caesar the things that are Caesar's.'

After the Passion the nascent Christian community was still part of Jewry. Its final separation was demonstrated in AD 66 when Christians refused to join in an uprising against Rome which was more social than religious. The early Christian congregations were composed of three classes, the hearers, the catechumens (those under instruction), and the baptized. The catechumens could not take part in the eucharist and candidates for baptism had to undergo a strict examination before the rite was administered to them. The fact that baptism and confirmation could only be administered once suggests that they were initiatic in intention, which enables us to equate them with the Lesser mysteries, while the sacrament of ordination corresponds to the Greater mysteries. There are many facts which bear witness to the esoteric nature of the New Testament, notably the fact that the eucharistic sacrament was received in two kinds, although nowadays the bread and wine in the Orthodox church are received by all the faithful.

Other signs of a teaching reserved for some can be found in the Letters of St Paul. 'I could not speak unto you as spiritual but as unto carnal . . . I have fed you with milk not with meat. . .' (1 Cor. 3: 1-2). The writings of the early Fathers allude to 'a truth which it is not permitted that the catechumens should contemplate'. St Basil writes even more explicitly of 'a silent and mystical tradition carried down even to us . . . secret teaching which our fathers obeyed for they had learned how necessary silence is to maintain respect for the mysteries'. A little later the writings of Dionysius speak of 'a secret which our inspired masters transmitted to their disciples, a kind of spiritual and almost heavenly instruction, initiating in the spirit and by the spirit . . . knowledge not made for everyone'.

But since it was Jewish in origin this new religion could only spread in the known world of its time by using Greek as its language. This symbiosis with a decadent Hellenism took place in Alexandria, the first modern capital city and meeting place of three cultures, Egyptian, Jewish, and Hellenistic. It is from here that Christianity no doubt acquired the principal elements of its vocabulary and its intellectual arguments. The Hermetic literature was believed by the Fathers of the Church, and long after them, to contain authentic relics of Egyptian theology inspired by Thoth, the Egyptian God of Wisdom, analogous to the Greek Hermes, the Jewish Enoch, and the Christian Logos. The Hermetic writings contain passages on contemplation worthy of Plotinus. Clement of Alexandria who before his baptism was familiar with the mystery religions, uses the same terminology when speaking of Christian initiation. 'I become sanctified when I am initiated . . . it is the Lord who is the hierophant (expounder of mysteries) . . . he places his seal on the adept. These are the "orgies" of our mysteries. Come and receive them.'

But Christianity could only retain its esoteric character by remaining hidden. Everything was changed when Constantine accepted it as the religion of the Empire and when he moved his capital to Byzantium. On emerging into the light of day the new doctrine was compelled to find a legal basis, which it did by deriving its canon law from the Roman legal system. The administrative framework of the Empire was used by the Church. This liaison with society was fatal; Christ never envisaged his teaching being given practical application since its instructions are inapplicable to 'the world' and must be interpreted as 'counsels of perfection'.

All that had originally been esoteric was now carefully concealed. The parables came to be regarded as simple moral tales; the inner truths which the average mind found hard to grasp became mysteries. The sacraments whilst retaining their value as symbols gradually lost their restricted character.

For the same reason Christian doctrine was inevitably distorted when its high spirituality was confronted by the exigencies of everyday life. The way of Christ seemed particularly difficult to follow and likely to expose its adherents to the risk of permanent hypocrisy, as Kierkegaard decided when he declared Christianity to be 'unliveable'.

So rationality took a hand, it laid hold of Greek philosophy and created scholasticism with its inevitable outcome; Cartesian rationalism. On the other hand, spiritual aspirations were satisfied thanks to sacerdotal initiation, monastic spirituality, and also through numerous Hermetic initiatory organizations, guilds, orders of chivalry, etc., which appeared in the West.

During this time Eastern Orthodox Christianity which knew nothing of scholasticism or the Reformation maintained its unbroken chain of spiritual teaching as witnessed to by the illustrious succession of Greek Fathers. Its development seems to have been more in the realm of method than of doctrine. For if sometimes the metaphysical aspect of a doctrine remains theoretical, its psychic and practical counterparts make its potential actual through the power of ritual.

8.

Orthodox Hesychasm

The word Hesychasm, derived from a Greek word meaning quiet, denotes in fact a complex state of silence, solitude, and peace. Its practice can be traced back to the Desert Fathers whose methods of prayer led finally to Hesychasm. The original centre from which it spread was Mount Sinai from whence, under the pressure of the Turkish invasion, it migrated to Mount Athos. From the 4th century onwards, following the example of St Anthony, anchorites had retired to hermitages in the deserts of Egypt and Cappadocia. They enjoyed great personal prestige and this was also accorded to their communities, to such an extent that the Eastern episcopate was always drawn from amongst the monks.

Evagrius Ponticus (346–399), disciple of St Macarius and friend of the great Cappadocian Fathers, fulfilled the role of initiator. Spiritual heir to Clement and Origen he was the first to develop a theory of pure prayer, prayer as a conversation between the intellect and God. His successors, Diadoch of Photikos, and St John of the Ladder (Climacus) brought into being a synthesis whose central part was the Jesus Prayer, in memory of his Holy Name. But although this unceasing prayer figures in the rule of St Basil and is also recommended in the rule of St John Cassian, the rule of St Benedict, which is the foundation of Western monasticism, does not mention it. There is no doubt that the founder of the Benedictines considered monastic discipline as the first stage of a life which would find its fulfilment in the state of an anchorite. While the Arab invasion was severing the West from its origins, the East was enlarging the scope of its method. St Simeon, the New Theologian, recommended that prayer should be as uninterrupted as breathing and the cardiac rhythm. 'Where the body is', he said, 'the mind should be also . . . The hesychast is a corporeal being who strives to bring his mind into his heart.'

By this he was implying a poetic mode of prayer like those other examples we have mentioned, the *nembutsu* of the Buddhists, the *dhikr* of the Sufis, the *japa* of the Yogis, of which the value is guaranteed by the Laws of Manu where it is written: 'A Brahmin may achieve blessedness by invocation alone, without any other ritual'. Even the West has not entirely neglected it. There is a trace of it to be found in St Ignatius Loyola's Spiritual Exercises in which he speaks of a 'third prayer by rhythm'.

In the Byzantine world pure prayer was based theologically on the writings of Gregory Palamas, Bishop of Thessalonika, who died in 1359. What had been up till then a method of prayer including a reserved rite became a doctrine to which a 'gnosis' was inseparably linked. Palamas had received his initiation into pure prayer from Theoleptus of Philadelphia which is in Lydia, and also during his time on Mount Athos, where he spent twenty years living the coenobitic life. Palamas opposed the exclusive spirituality of the Platonists with the biblical teaching that the body is not a prison for the soul but a temple, because since Christ's incarnation it has been the means of manifesting the Holy Spirit. The system of prayer of the Hesychasts realized the potential of this connection between soul and body. The heart is the dwelling place of the Divine and the body ought to pray in union with the heart. Palamas restored the body to its rightful position, at the same moment that the alchemists in the West were doing the same thing: 'To each according to their own law and due. For the body, temperance, for the soul, charity, for the reason, moderation, and for the spirit, prayer.'

This recognition of the immanence of the spirit in the body (the temple of the Holy Ghost) enlightens and completes the negative teaching which Dionysius the pseudo-Areopagite had revived in the 5th century. Dionysius did not put forward any means of reconciling conflicting texts which described the Divinity in its two-fold aspect of inaccessibility and yet capability of being communicated with. Palamas threw light on this dilemma in his dialogue *Theophanes*. God is inaccessible and beyond our power to communicate with by our reason (by virtue of His 'non-being') but by virtue of His 'being' He may be known by the heart through His works, His energies, His attributes, which Dionysius calls virtues and Gregory Nazianus His *élans*, and what Thomists call uncreated grace. But whereas in the West this Grace is an 'accident' in which we share without knowing it, in the East it is considered as being an inherent part of the redeemed nature. Grace and freedom are no longer in opposition and Gregory of Nyssa sees in them the two faces of the one single reality which unites the human will with the Divine. The true Hesychast unites immanence and transcendence the two extremes of all spirituality. Evagrius Ponticus explains this union in a formula worthy of India. 'The vision of God is one with the vision of the Self. But it should be remembered that this way of prayer is subject to the preparation of the body by fasting and vigil. As Palamas says: 'It is the narrow way since it can only be effective when based on those virtues which predispose the soul to union.'

In 1782 under the title of *Philokalia* a collection of texts on the Prayer of the Heart from the writings of the Greek Fathers and edited by the Bishop of Corinth and a monk from Mount Athos was published in Venice. The word *Philokalia* or Love of Beauty had already been used by St Basil for his anthology on the writings of the great Platonist Origen. The *Philokalia*, which was disseminated widely among the hermitages of the Russian *startzi* and translated for popular use, has maintained its spiritual influence to the present time and has been translated into English and many other languages. Its teachings have been given a new dimension in the works of Soloviev, Chestov, Bulgakov, Berdyaev, and Lossky.

9.

Knights Templar, Fedeli d'Amore, and The Rose-Cross

The esoteric teaching which took refuge in the East with the hermits and in the West with the religious orders was obliged to borrow from them their means of restricting the dissemination of their teaching to those capable of receiving it and even to use secrecy as a means of survival. It is very difficult to discover more than confirmatory hints of their survival from parallel inferences. Only the vicissitudes of history compel initiatic organizations to come into the open, where they are confronted by official religion which tends to ignore them and with the powers that be, which condemn them, for governments, like individuals, fear what they do not understand. It is the interrupted film of these appearances which we will try to unroll before the reader. We will at the same time try to discover the order of their succession, their interchanging membership, and their degree of authenticity.

The essential cause of the decline of initiatic organizations is due to the rupture of the links that bind them one with another and each one of them to the centre. The schism between the Eastern and Western branches of Christianity and the Arab blockade of the Mediterranean prevented that ease of interchange which the Crusades aimed at reestablishing. This role of intermediary was filled by the new Order of Knights Templars founded in 1119 between the first and second Crusades. This was a moment when there was no longer any question of fighting but rather of consolidating the conquest and of bringing peace to the new Christian Kingdom. The Statutes of the Order were revised and approved by St Bernard of Clairvaux, who wished to act as godfather to an ideal order of Christian chivalry whose members would assume the responsibility of being guardians of the Holy Land. All chivalric initiation possesses by definition an esoteric character, but the title given to the new Order was particularly revealing. In the

Western world where the Judaeo-Christian tradition was dominant, an Order which took as its emblem the Temple of Solomon would be seen to be aware of the unity at the higher level of the three religions which acknowledged Abraham as their father. Naturally, the members of the Order would have had other relations with the Muslims of the new kingdom than warlike ones. In fact, in Jerusalem the Templars occupied the El Aksa mosque and for more than a century were in daily contact with the Arabs.

Furthermore, as these Knights were members of a religious order, their name 'guardians of the Holy Land' assumed a higher meaning. We know that each of the different authentic Traditions has its own Holy Land, counterpart of the ideal Holy Land, symbol of the Primordial Tradition itself. In the case of the Templars the city of Jerusalem was not only the centre of Mosaic tradition but also the image of the spiritual state for which it stood. We can easily understand how in these conditions the temporal and regal power was alarmed by a fraternization between Christians and Muslims which transcended all doctrinal differences. This carried to extremes resulted in the 'cupidity' condemned by Dante, and this in turn resulted in the condemnation of the Order by Rome, an event which, according to one's point of view, may be described as a scandal or as inevitable.

Many important manifestations of esoteric doctrines coincided with the destruction of the Order of Knights Templars. Christian and Muslim initiates came to an agreement to maintain their links which had been broken. This unseen reorganization succeeded thanks to the members of groups such as the Fede Santa, the Fedeli d'Amore, and the Rose-Cross, who prudently never assumed any definite organized status. As René Guénon points out, there are in the City Museum in Vienna two medals, one with the portrait of Dante and the other with the portrait of the painter Pisanello. Both medals bear on the back the inscription: F.S.K.I.P.F.T., which should be interpreted as follows: *Fidei Sanctae Kadosch Imperialis Principatus Frater Templarius*. This association, the Fede Santa, of which Dante appears to have been one of the leaders, was a third order with Templar affiliations whose dignitaries were known as Kadosch (holy or set apart). It is not by chance Guénon continues, that Dante at the end of his journey in *The Divine Comedy* takes St Bernard, who had established the Rule of the Templars, as his guide. In doing so it is as if he wished to indicate that the spirituality of St Bernard was the only means for knights of chivalry to attain to the highest place in the spiritual hierarchy.

Moreover, the structure of *The Divine Comedy* is based on a framework of esoteric symbolism. It is now many years since the Spanish priest Father Asin Palacios showed that two very important sources of *The Divine Comedy* were in fact two Muslim mystical texts, *The Book of the Ladder* and *The Book of the Night Voyage*. Again we can see that the seven heavens in the poem are also echoed in the seven initiatic stages of the Fedeli d'Amore, another group to which Dante and many other of his poet friends belonged. The Lady in their poetry stood for Divine Wisdom or Transcendent Intelligence, their *Cuore gentile* was the noble heart purified from worldly constraints. The members of the Fedeli d'Amore wrote in verse, the language of the angels and the gods. Boccacio who was a member of the fraternity has revealed its esoteric transcendence in one of the novels of his *Decameron* when he makes Melchizedek say 'that between Judaism, Christianity, and Islam no one could determine which was the true faith'.

It can be reasonably assumed that the Rosicrucians were the heirs of the Fede Santa, although they never revealed themselves in any exoteric form. The term Rose-Cross designates a spiritual state comprising knowledge of cosmology related to hermetic Christian beliefs. One of their most noteworthy characteristics was 'the gift of tongues', that is, the capability of speaking to everyone in his own language. They adopted the habits and customs of all the countries they passed through, even adopting a new name; they were cosmopolitans in the true meaning of the word. In 1614 the German alchemist Valentine Weigel published the legend of the founder, Christian Rosencreutz, and his symbolic voyages, thus making public the existence of the Fraternity. When we remember that Luther's personal seal bore a cross in the centre of a rose and that most of those who were called Rosicrucians were Lutheran alchemists, such as Khunrath, Maier, and Robert Fludd, one can deduce that the public appearance of this society is an apparently esoteric episode in the history of the Reformation. It may also be noted as a curiosity that Leibniz put a rose with five petals in the centre of a cross at the head of his book *De Arte Combinatoria*, in which he deals with the question of a universal language, and that Descartes tried in vain, as he himself relates, to get in touch with a society bearing this name. It is said that the Rosicrucians left Europe for India at the beginning of the 17th century, which can be seen as the reabsorption of the society into an Eastern centre. In any event, modern Rosicrucians have no true effectual links with the true Rose-Cross and whoever claims to be one is by that fact not one.

10.
Hermetic Cosmology

The primitive Christian tradition was not concerned with science in the modern sense of the word, and the Gospels do not specify any special legal code nor do they teach any particular cosmological system. The early Christians were necessarily the inheritors of contemporary Hellenistic science. Esoteric teaching in order to make itself comprehensible naturally made use of the vocabulary of the arts, sciences, and trades then existent, and its ritualized symbols drawn from them were also used in the initiation of members of those trades. As Christian Hermetism of necessity used the Greek language, it was the result of a symbiosis of evangelical and Jewish spirituality and Alexandrian cosmology. It included two systems of knowledge then much in favour, astrology and alchemy, both of which sprang from sacerdotal initiation. We should remember that ancient educationalists gave the name 'liberal arts' to two distinct divisions of knowledge, a division which persisted up to the Middle Ages. There was the science of letters or *trivium*, to which alchemy was related and which included grammar, logic, and rhetoric, and then there was the science of numbers of *quadrivium*, which included arithmetic, geometry, astrology, and music.

In studying alchemy and astrology separately we are inclined to forget that there is a link between them which stems from their common presupposition of cosmic oneness. Between astrology, which is concerned with the heavenly world of planetary spheres, and alchemy, which deals with the earthly world and natural states, there exists a relationship which one could define by saying that astrology represents 'the will of Heaven' and alchemy represents 'the progressive will of man', a duality of forces which it is the objective of initiation to unite.

Today astrology suffers when it survives in a debased form as mere prediction, and as such it is justifiably condemned. René Guénon has said: 'The so-called astrological traditions represent the debris of a science long lost and no longer understood.' It is also worth noting that those astrological works which are known today belong to periods of the decadence of tradition, namely the end of Greek antiquity with Ptolemy and the end of the Renaissance with Morin de Villefranche. In reality the importance of astrology lies in its teaching something which is found nowhere else, namely, the science of cosmic cycles and 'qualified time'.

In our world every phenomenon is made manifest by the movement which links them and thus through the rhythm which controls this movement. The celestial bodies demonstrate this rhythm in its pure form and this is why they form the basis of mathematics, astrologers having been the first mathematicians, a name given to them by the Pythagoreans. As all rhythm presupposes a returning cycle, astrology was the science of cycles and of 'qualified time'. The permanence of natural laws, which modern science has reduced to mere formulas, implies, in accordance with science, the quasi-eternal stability of the conditions in which these laws operate. But the traditional theory of cycles on the contrary assumes a continuous change, a growing acceleration of time as the world grows farther and farther away from its original starting point. This is accompanied by a corresponding degeneration in every realm. By their orderliness and symbolism cycles admirably illustrate the variation in the qualitative nature of time and the transformation of the cosmic environment into which man is being continuously thrust. Each cycle can thus both symbolize a different spiritual state and a given moment in history.

This cosmic environment is not only that in which man finds himself but is also that of the whole of nature. The teachings of alchemy say in effect that each planet marks with its 'sign' a different metal created within the terrestrial matrix. Ancient science taught that, under the celestial influence of the sun and the planets, the original *prima materia* 'ripened' slowly and gave rise to a series of metals of progressively valuable quality, culminating in the perfection of gold. The alchemist in his laboratory aimed at imitating the operations of nature. By means of the fire in his furnace or *athanor*, in which the fiery principle took the place of the sun, he aimed to accomplish in the forty days of an alchemical gestation what nature accomplished in the forty weeks of a human gestation period.

It is easy to understand how esoteric teaching made use of this symbolism based as it was on the concept of cosmic unity, without, however, being bound to it any more than it is bound to any other of the ancient scientific notions which seem to us to be outdated. All that is, arises from the same substance, and the whole cosmos may be considered as one vast organism animated by one life-giving principle. The progressive states in the transmutation of matter in alchemy can be seen to be the equivalent of the different stages of purification in any initiatic system. Alchemy revealed the process by which life regains the original purity of the undifferentiated *prima materia* of which it is formed. Thus we can see that initiatic process and 'the great work' of alchemy are one and the same; the victory of light, as a stage on the way towards the symbolic perfection of gold, which according to the Vedas *is* immortality. One can also say that astrology is a clock measuring the qualitative nature of time which enables alchemy to be used as a therapeutic agent in the different stages. Both astrology and alchemy are in perfect correspondence with each other and both derive from Christian hermetic teaching whose language was used by the alchemists.

11.

Guilds and Freemasonry

Between the light of Heaven and the darkness of Earth the realm of cosmology includes the surface of the inhabited world. It thus gives rise to the notion of a 'sacred geography' which determines the choice of propitious places for human habitation and the building of towns. As all civilization and all other arts are dominated by the art of architecture, so architecture is intimately associated with the creation of towns, which at the beginning of the medieval period included within their walls the artisans who were dependent on the feudal and monastic estates.

Every craft which had a traditional character could act as a means of initiation. Legend insists that all arts, sciences, and trades are the result of a divine initiative, prototype of all subsequent craft initiation. The Roman god Janus was, we know, both the patron of all trades and of the mysteries, and in Greek legend the Titan-demiurge Prometheus was the teacher of those techniques which enabled men to master the art of fire, manual labour, and also eloquence, poetry, and music.

In the West two organizations which originated with craft fraternities have survived up to the present, no doubt in a somewhat reduced state but with their rich symbolism of craft initiation still intact. They are Guildry (*Compagnonnage*) and Masonry, which through its architectural symbolism is related to cosmology.

By the beginning of the age of Charlemagne (*c*. AD 750) workmen's associations, which were the successors to the *collegia fabrorum* of Roman times, had adopted the form of religious fraternities. The brother-companions, who practised those basic crafts related to architecture, travelled from workshop to workshop and were thus everywhere treated as 'strangers' and 'transients' with the qualifications which they had preserved in the different rites of their respective trades. Isolated in their lodges these masons, shapers of the stones which built the cathedrals, drew together in closed communities which only admitted members of the same profession.

For what is remarkable about the guilds is that they have retained their secret character and their original community spirit. Each one of their rites is placed under the patronage of an historical or mythical personage, King Solomon, Master James, and Père Soubise, for if the legend originally referred to the building of the Temple in Jerusalem, it was later Christianized. These three personages in fact represent the three castes, the royal, the artisanal, and the sacerdotal. And guildry in spite of its community sense has kept this tripartite division of aspirant, companion, and master.

Its rites of initiation include both strenuous trade tests and episodes from the life of Christ as symbolized in the Mass. This was the pretext for its condemnation between the 15th and 17th centuries when it emerged from obscurity into the light of history. At this time the rites were not properly understood and were deemed to be sacriligious parodies, whereas in fact they were the survival of a Christianized Jewish tradition. The legend of the foundation of the Temple in Jerusalem relates that after it was finished its master architect, Hiram, was assassinated by three jealous companions and buried in a tomb of brass in the Temple itself. This dramatic story may be compared with the end of a *chanson de geste* of the 13th century by Renaud de Montauban. In it we read that the beloved youngest son of Aymon returning from the Holy Land in pilgrim's dress, hired himself to the workshop of Cologne Cathedral where he was assassinated by three jealous companions.

These sacrificial rites connected with the foundation of a building can perhaps be illuminated by reference to the ancient precedents provided by the human sacrifices which accompanied the foundation of Vedic sanctuaries.

The close resemblance of the symbolism of Guilds and Freemasonry leads one to think that they have a common origin. It is said that the name Freemason is derived from the freedom from taxes granted by the emperor in 1276 to the workmen at Strasbourg Cathedral; this at least is the legendary origin of the fraternity. These Frei-Maurer or Freemasons would have founded the first Lodge (*Bauhutte*) of the Holy Roman Empire. This was followed by other Lodges in Vienna, Cologne, and Zurich. Two centuries later in 1459 the Master of Works at Strasbourg had united the German Lodges in a Federation which it seems regularized all the rites at a meeting in Ratisbonne. The same granting of communal liberties promoted in England and France the reunion of

Lodges which could have been in existence for a very long time, indeed, there are some who claim that they go back as far as the Roman workmen's fraternities.

The Lodge with its star-studded ceiling represents the world. The partial stripping of those applying for membership recalls the experiences of aspirants in the mystery religions. The initiate undergoes the initiatic death in the darkened room and then is reborn into the light; walks and journeys represent the various trials.

In the 17th century a modification of former practices took place which seems to us something entirely new. Lodges received non-professional masons, known as 'accepted', especially priests, who were initiated into special Lodges to take the position of chaplains. All were members of the same masonic group which operated within the Christian Church itself. For reasons which are by no means clear, the number of 'accepted' masons increased, especially in England, no doubt to allow the reception of members of other organizations which were persecuted or proscribed. Lodges were full of intellectuals and members of the aristocracy, who were received into the grade of master. In the 17th century the number of operative masons practising their trade was greatly reduced in many Lodges and operative masonry had degenerated into specula-tive masonry. When in 1689 King James Stuart took refuge at the court of Louis XIV, it is possible that Scottish noblemen in his entourage founded Lodges which may have been the origin of the 'Scottish Rite' which was especially prominent in France.

Up to this point all is hypothetical. The starting point of modern masonry is England at the beginning of the 18th century. The Rev. James Anderson, Chaplain of the St Paul's Lodge in London, and the Frenchman J. T. Desaguliers, who was Chaplain to the Prince of Wales, collected together a number of masons, supporters of the House of Orange, and between 1714 and 1717 elaborated a new ritual whose inspiration was Protestant, after which it is said they burnt the archives because they were tainted with Papism. The Grand Lodge of England of accepted masons based on Ander-son's Constitutions was founded in 1723 with the Duke of Whar-ton as Grand Master. This took place in spite of the protests of other Lodges, including that of York which claimed great antiq-uity. In 1735 the French Lodges made a Scottish baronet, J. H. Maclean, their Grand Master, and it was not until 1738 that these so-called English Lodges freed themselves from English supervi-sion and the Duc d'Antin was elected Grand Master of the new *Loge de France*.

It comes as no surprise to learn that Trade Guilds were condemned by the Sorbonne in 1655 and 1791 by the Constituent Assembly, as Masonry had been by the Holy See in 1738 and 1751. But the numerous repetitions of such bans prove their inefficacy. The greatest noblemen of France were masons, including the most illustrious proponent of Papal authority, Joseph de Maistre, who rightly said: 'All agree that Freemasony is a branch, detached and perhaps corrupted, of an ancient and respectable stock.' And he adds: 'True religion is a great deal older than eighteen hundred years. It came into being with time itself.'

12.

Master Eckhart and Nicholas of Cusa

From its Apostolic beginnings and throughout the Middle Ages Christian spirituality had its adherents in all types of organization, both initiatic and mystical. It did not realize or claim that it was esoteric, even when sometimes it was. They come to light from time to time as small very restricted groups, such as those of the Beguins and Beghards of the 13th century or in the writings of the mystics, who should be considered as inheritors and not initiators of a tradition. Amongst them we find dedicated priests, authentic freemasons, great mystics, and simple 'inspired' souls. We name them because otherwise the continuity of their method, the identical nature of their goal, and the persistence of the need, would be difficult to grasp. The apparent variation of form does not arise from the underlying doctrine which is always the same but from differences of language and of those who use it.

The German Rhineland, that 'street of saints', *die Pfaffengasse*, has become part of the spiritual history of the Middle Ages. And it will remain part of history, although it is difficult to evaluate with any certainty the quality of the sources from which so many original figures from Albertus Magnus to Schelling have drawn.

In Eckhart, for example, the strength of his conviction was such that it led him to use expressions which succeeded in alarming the hierarchy. He shared the same Dominican habit with St Thomas Aquinas but, against the Angelic Doctor's view that God is unknowable only because of the weakness of our understanding, he maintained that God is unknowable and ineffable in Himself. The Supreme Deity has no name. He is neither Goodness nor Wisdom, nor Spirit nor Essence, nor Person nor Image. Above all reigns the Deity who only in His relationship with man can become God. On the spiritual plane the Deity is identical with that uncreated part of the soul which he called a 'something' (*etwas*) or 'a strong castle', a 'citadel', a 'spark', an 'uncreated ark'. Eckhart was a mystic who brought to his intuition a verbal felicity amounting to genius, creating images which scandalized those who set themselves up as judges and which were thus bound to be exoteric in their nature. He saw the just man transformed into the divine essence as the bread in the Eucharist is transformed into the Body of Christ. He reckoned that 'consciousness of union with God was the last hindrance to perfect blessedness. The truly noble man should be freed even from God Himself, or all knowledge of God, so that absolute emptiness should be his state'.

A century later Nicholas of Cusa, a cardinal in the Roman Church, in his *Apologia*, sought to justify himself and his predecessors Plotinus, Dionysius the Areopagite, and Eckhart. For him too God in his pure essence is inaccessible. But since he was more an intellectual than a mystic, his method of approaching the ineffable was 'the art of geometrical transmutations'. For him ideas and concepts are not static; at the extreme limit of its development each concept coincides with its opposite. For him explanation is not to be found by consulting a table of fixed values or universal types, but by finding a mathematical formula which will transform an obscure intuition into a rational function. Understanding has as its role the reconciling of contradictions and if this is possible, it is so because there is in our souls a reflection of the Divine Essence. God is more within man than he is himself. Truth is no longer the ultimate objective of prolonged thought processes, but the recognition within the depths of the individual's soul of an unfathomable infinity. The observer is always, like the modern relativist, at the centre. In space he creates his order and his hierarchy. Time, the unchanging present in which he lives, is a reflexion of eternity. In all modes of being Nicholas of Cusa saw a sharing in what can never be shared.

It is not surprising that he longed for a unity of all religions in accordance with the primordial tradition. In his formulation of religion he was so abstract that everyone could subscribe to it. He wrote a *Critical Examination of the Q'uran*, and he went to Constantinople to try to reconcile the Byzantine Emperor to the See of Rome. He urged the Pope to write a letter to the Turkish Sultan offering him the succession to the Eastern Emperors. For Nicholas of Cusa 'revelations' were numerous and dogmas and rites consisted of partial truths. As he poignantly declared: 'They call on You by a variety of Holy Names, for You are as You are and You remain You, unknowable and ineffable'. He passed from the transcendence of a negative theoology to the immanence of the infinite presence. His *Docta Ignorantia* (Learned Ignorance) achieves the transcendence of contradictions. But he knew that the profane are not capable of understanding the treasure they bear within them. True knowledge is esoteric and Nicholas Cusa proclaimed this in a splendid way: 'Wisdom cries in the public places and what she cries is that she dwells on the mountain-tops'.

13.

Theosophists

Although the Reformation was very far from being in any way esoteric, it did nevertheless, indirectly and as it were functionally, meet certain aspirations of this kind. This explains how certain figures as exceptional as Jacob Boehme could flourish, especially in the early years after the Reformation. He arose as a truly inspired figure, endowed with a gift for language, amongst medical alchemists and astrologers, heirs of Paracelsus who lived somewhat outside official reformed circles. He made use of the hermetic terminology. Alone in the West he and Gichtel knew of and used the notion of psychic centres in man. With Eckhart he spoke of the Eternal Birth of the Son and of deification through the Word. Hence his concept of the *Ungrund*, the undetermined abyss, corresponding to metaphysical Non-being. He belonged to that long line of thinkers who, when faced with the immutability of scholastic logic, extolled the systematic growth of the Wisdom within us, a notion which as Nicholas Berdyaev was fond of saying, corresponds closely to the Orthodox *Sophia*.

What Boehme tried in his own language to explain was how and why the Deity became the Creator. He found it difficult to explain because for him the Creator was the great mystery, the *Mysterium Magnum*. He was inspired to reveal the emergence of all the hypostases or manifestations of the Abyssal Ungrund because this Ungrund is absolute liberty or, as Leibniz and Guénon called it, Universal Possibility. Jacob Boehme, like the later German metaphysicians, put great emphasis on the active fecundity of the Possible, of which, as we have seen, Wisdom is the first hypostasis. Wisdom's nature is dual for it is image and likeness of the Deity in itself, and of the Divine in man. It is by nature androgynous, which was recognized by hermetic cosmology. All creation shows signs of contraries in opposition and therein can

be found the different 'signatures' of all things which Man recon-
ciles within himself. Through Wisdom and the signatures of all
things (Boehme's *Signatura Rerum*)man is both image of the world
and an image of God.

The spirit of Eckhart to which Boehme was heir also inspired
the lyrical impulse of Angelus Silesius, friend of Abraham Franken-
berg, Boehme's friend, first editor, and biographer. Angelus Silesius'
path was that of love and its means of expression poetical lyri-
cism. In his verses he delighted in revealing the contradictory,
often shocking nature of truth: 'God can do nothing without me',
'God is pure nothing', 'I am like God and God is like me'. Such
antitheses appear at first sight to be facile but they are laden with
meaning, echoing the spirit of Boehme and resonating on down
a long line to the 19th century Romantics.

14.

Tradition and Romanticism

Throughout the 17th century and the Age of Enlightenment a secret chain of spiritually enlightened men, if not actual initiates, linked the Platonists of the Renaissance, Marsilio Ficino, Pico de Mirandola, Giordano Bruno, and Tommaso Campanella, to the first Romantic movement. The quality of the men who formed this chain was not always certain, and there are some whose claims are suspect. The humanism of the 17th and 18th centuries was inferior to that of the 16th. The nobleman was no longer a 'microcosm' but a sceptic. Romanticism was a reaction against rationalism and its offspring revolutionary atheism.

In France the renewal of the feeling for religion and tradition found its theoreticians in those 'prophets of the past', Le Vicomte Louis de Bonald, J. de Maistre, and L. C. de Saint-Martin. In Germany the same sentiment gave rise to the creation in Masonry of a hierarchy of high grades in imitation of the Orders of Chivalry. The Templar Rite of the Strict Observance was founded in 1754 by Baron de Hundt filled by nostalgia for the Holy Roman Empire, inspired by the grandeurs of Germany in the Middle Ages. About the same time in Lyons, Martinez de Pasqualy, a Freemason of Spanish origin, founded the Order of Elect Cohens in order to have a vehicle for putting into practice his own programme of self-realization which he described in his great work *Traité de la Réintegration des Êtres*. When de Pasqualy left France for the West Indies, two of his disciples, L. C. de Saint-Martin and J. B. Willermoz developed in Lodges in Lyons and Wilhelmsbad (1782) the constitutions of a Rectified Scottish Rite which was recognized by the main body of French Freemasons of the Grand Orient Lodge and incorporated the Elect Cohens.

The most outstanding figure of this new era was undoubtedly the Comte Joseph de Maistre. He became a master at the age of

twenty-one and was a great orator and ardent believer. He soon
became, as had the Tsar Alexander the First, a 'Beneficent Knight
of the Holy City', which was the highest grade in the Rectified
Scottish Rite. De Maistre was also a Catholic of the most intran-
sigent kind and the author of a treatise on *The Pope* in which he
declared 'Christianity in its early days was a truly initiatory system', and he answered his critics by saying that 'What was clear
to those in the know (adepts) was unintelligible to the rest of
mankind'. Before Bonald and his numerous imitators, de Maistre
was the leader of the French school of Traditionalists, the fore-
runners of the Romantic movement. But he remained in true
French style too much of a humanist to have much influence in
Europe which was dominated at that time by German intellectual ideas. In sharp contrast to him, his friend Louis-Claude de
Saint-Martin (le Philosophe Inconnu), who was more of a mystic
than an initiate, fervent admirer of Boehme and student of Sweden-
borg, was much read in Germany where Herder in 1773 had begun
the process of reassessing the Middle Ages. Other protestants such
as J. G. Hamann (*The Magus of the North*), Starck, and Jacobi all
stood out against the prevailing rationalism of *Die Aufklarung* or
Enlightenment. They were followed by Catholic and other sym-
pathizers like F. von Baader, Z. Werner, F. von Schlegel, and his
friends Novalis, Tieck, and Schelling. They were all adherents of
the great German tradition of Eckhart and Boehme, a tradition
based on the concept of 'the All' according to which 'The Universal'
alone can have any significance. Analogical symbolism rejected
by Cartesians gained a new hearing thanks to the work of Friedrich
Creuzer, J. J. von Gorres, and Franz Brentano. The rise of the
Catholic renewal and its fusion with the Teutonic spirit restored
to the Holy Roman Empire its former preeminence as the most
perfect form of balance between the spiritual and the temporal
powers. The dominating idea of the elite in Germany in the
Romantic era was that of the regeneration of mankind by means
of an occult society of intellectuals and initiates. A manifesto to
this end was published by Novalis, the poet and philosopher, called
Europe or Christianity (1799) in which he attacked Lutheranism
for having impoverished Christian thought by reducing it to a
Biblical literalism and because it had destroyed European unity.
Romanticism substituted a sense of mystery for the narrow rationalism of the philosophers. It appeared as the driving force behind
a burgeoning spirituality which has not yet been fully understood.

15.

The Oriental Renaissance

A further step in the Romantic Movement gave rise to a renewed
interest in Oriental thought. It is true that the name of the Buddha
was not unknown to Clement of Alexandria, and Hippolytus of
Rome quotes from the Vedas. But fifteen hundred years had to
pass before they reappeared in the West with any chance of being
understood by a civilization long the heir of a decadent Hellenism
and filled with classical prejudice. The humanists could not conceive of a cradle civilization other than the Egyptian, nor of any
other viaduct which could lead them back to their origins than
the Bible or Pythagoras. This attitude of mind led them to seek
the sources of the Primordial Tradition in Hellenism and to believe
that Hebrew was the language of God. This error was perpetu-
ated in the 18th century by such writers as Court de Gebelin,
the young Schlegel, and by Fabre d'Olivet; the work of this latter
writer is however worthy of respect. He may have confused
Pythagoras and Moses but he learned Arabic and Hebrew and
buried himself in the study of the book of Genesis. His many years
of study resulted in his major work *La Langue Hebraique restituée*,
in which he revealed the universal meaning of the sacred text.
There is no doubt that his linguistic ideas were frequently wrong
but it was not in fact the roots of Hebrew words which provided
him with the fundamental features of the system of thought he
derived from them, but on the contrary it was his genius as a
metaphysical thinker that helped out over and over again the weaknesses of the linguist.

It is unfortunate that he did not take note of the fact that in
1771 Anquetil-Duperron had begun to translate the *Avesta* and
had introduced the first Upanishads into France, about which he
said they 'present the same truths as the Platonists, who may
perhaps have learnt them from the East'. When Fabre d'Olivet him-

self wished to use the English translation of the *Ramayana* his prejudices as a former supporter of the revolution led him to invert the order of the Ages of the World and to remove the Golden Age from its place at the beginning and to place it at the end.

Only the authentic Tradition of the East would be able to liberate Europe from its Greek and modernistic prejudices by enabling it to discover the essential doctrinal unity of all the religions of humanity. The first step towards this was taken by English Indologists. From 1785 onwards a series of direct translations from the Sanskrit was undertaken by Sir William Jones, founder of the Bengal Asiatic Society. His work was carried on by H. T. Colebrooke, whose Essay on the Vedas was published in 1805 and translated into French by Pauthier in 1833.

On their side the Germans welcomed with fervour the opportunity these texts presented them with for freeing themselves from their hated dependence on classicism. Following Colebrooke, F. von Schlegel wrote *On the Language and Wisdom of the Hindus* (1808). The group centered on Heidelberg of Creuzer, Tieck, Goerres, and Brentano read the papers printed in *Asiatic Researches* as a providential revelation. For in them they saw the proof of Schelling's contention that there was 'a Christianity before History'. However, the acceptance of the sort of Christianity taught by Boehme could not help being very slow in Europe as a whole. Its reception demanded the sort of objectivity only given to it by Eugue Burnouf and Silvestre de Sacy. The School of Oriental Languages was started in 1795, a chair of Sanskrit in the College de France was founded in 1814, and *Le Journal Asiatique* began publication in 1823. These revelations of a very exalted spirituality were enthusiastically received by Lamartine and Michelet and stimulated what Edgar Quinet in his *Génie des Religions* called an 'Oriental renaissance'.

The widening of intellectual horizons in the Europe of 1848 provoked a reaction on the part of nationalist organizations, who were quick to take umbrage. German scholars substituted the word 'Indo-Germanic' for the formerly accepted 'Indo-European' and used linguistics in a racist way. The English, more interested in economic imperialism than in Sanskrit metaphysics, soon abandoned serious scholarly research in favour of a Theosophy inspired by political and protestant ideals. Rome itself took fright when it saw Oriental texts being compared with Christian scriptures and finally condemned Bonnetty, editor of the *Annales de Philosophie chrétienne* and friend of Montalembert and the Abbé Gerbet. In his periodical Bonetty had defended the principle of a primitive revelation and published Chinese and Biblical texts in parallel. M. R. Schwab summed the matter up correctly when he said: 'The Oriental renaissance threatened to degenerate into a war of religions'.

Roman caution is all the more comprehensible when we understand that instead of being confronted with true Eastern spirituality, it faced the intrusion of a distorted Orientalism which gave support to anti-Catholic propaganda and gave rise to that ignoble counterfeit known as Occultism. This modern movement stems largely from the work of a former deacon, A. L. Constant, better known under his pseudonym Eliphas Levi Zahed; his work has no authentic Eastern origins. But although he mixed facts with a great deal of fantasy in works such as *The Key of the Mysteries* and *Transcendental Magic; its Doctrine and Ritual*, he was vastly superior to the horde of baneful plagiarists, amongst whom there were Westernized Orientalists, all of whose propagandist efforts increased from 1870 onwards.

Such people under whatever name they operate, Theosophists, Anthroposophists, neo-Martinists, neo-Gnostics, Spiritualists, or Rosicrucians, are all exclusively concerned with 'phenomena' or happenings, which is absolutely foreign to any true metaphysic. The conditions which prevail in the world today favour such subversive and anti-traditional activity. The confusion between the spiritual and the psychic and the identification of the spiritual with what is most inferior in the psyche, the identification of religion with magic, totemism, and even sorcery, the popular dissemination of pseudo- or counter-initiatic rituals are all irrefutable examples of a degraded perversion of the truth. The growing materialism of our modern world, its increasing mechanization, and the current vogue for extreme artificiality, the virtual brainwashing or standardization of thought by the media, all reveal a mounting tide of uncontrolled and uncontrollable influences working on those who have practically no idea of their existence.

Tradition teaches that it is inevitable that at the end of each cycle all the detritus of past ages should be made use of. All that Ancient civilizations rejected, such as industrial machinery, not only because they mistrusted its enslaving nature and in respect for the existing division of labour by caste, but also because of a justifiable fear of the backlash of lower powers whose threat we are well able to appreciate today.

For a long time Indians did not bother to reply to the caricatures of their tradition disseminated by Westerners. But finally the worsening political consequences of such misunderstanding at last encouraged them to make the effort to contact those Europeans who might be able to help avoid a danger for the whole world, especially for those in the West who were prey to these misconceptions, by redressing the balance in favour of the true understanding of Hindu thought. Their early endeavours had little success. About 1886 they contacted a French nobleman, Le Marquis de Saint-Yves d'Alveydre, author of *La Mission des Juifs* (1884). He had acquired the papers of the mystic and scholar Antoine Fabre d'Olivet and had made very improper use of them. His Hindu contacts soon realized that he was only willing to make use of their teaching in order to forward his own personal political ideas and the initiative again failed. It was not until about 1908 that a new effort was made and resulted in the work of René Guénon.

Guénon (1886–1951) spent twenty years investigating various occult and spiritualist groups whose pretensions to esoteric knowledge had attracted him. He discovered that their pretensions to be able to provide him with sure and certain knowledge were false. He did however also associate himself with genuinely Oriental organizations. Even more exceptionally, the initiative from the East mentioned above enabled him to have close relations with the three principal Oriental traditions from the age of twenty-four onwards. He learned Sanskrit and in 1921 he began his work by publishing his *Introduction to Hindu Doctrines*, a work which in the depth and clarity of its metaphysical exposition was something entirely new in the West.

Thanks to his profound understanding of the Hindu, Muslim, and Chinese traditions, he reintroduced over and above theological and philosophical conceptions of Being the supra-personal concepts of the Infinite, Non-Being, and Universal Possibility. This restoration of a missing element in philosophy enabled him to revive the concept of the Primordial Revelation. This latter concept is by no means unknown to Christian thought. It can be found in the writings of Joseph de Maistre, who affirmed that 'there is no doctrine which is not rooted in man's inmost nature and in a tradition as old as humanity'. This understanding enabled Guénon to extend the notion of orthodoxy to all the various traditions without belittling the significance of their special features.

Then, leaving the Absolute and coming down to the level of human nature and the world of manifestation, he reintroduced to us the concept of the indefinite multiplicity and simultaneity of all states of being. He revealed that their realization was possible by means of direct and immediate consciousness, the attainment of which was facilitated by initiation. He never flattered himself that there was anything original in his teaching — very much the reverse. Like the Scholastics of the Middle Ages, and even more decisively, he was the restorer of an ancient truth and tradition which it has been the intention of this work to expound as adequately as possible.

Our age is seeking a universal understanding which men of vision can already foresee and which is the longing of all great souls. There is ample evidence that the world's economic problems can be solved without the different religions having to abandon their unique spiritual insights; after all, brotherly agreement does not prevent the individual growth of each member of the family, bodily separate, but united in heart and mind.

For esotericism is just this: the heart and mind of religions; it demonstrates that they are the offspring of one and the same Tradition. The blessing of Abraham is given still to his separated children. Buddhists and Hindus spring from the one Mother India, which is shared by Islam and Hinduism. Under varying names all acknowldge the one truth, which in the silence of the Mysteries filled those old initiates with Wisdom and which still today is inscribed over the entrance to our Christian monasteries with the most gracious name: Peace.

16.

The Tradition in Great Britain

by Robin Waterfield

In Great Britain the Reformation, the Dissolution of the Monsteries, and the emergence of a National Church headed by the reigning monarch, meant that the continuity of tradition was irretrievably lost and only very fragmentary traces of it remain accessible to us.

The early history of the primordial tradition in England is hidden in the monastic life of the time. It emerges into the light of history in the persons of Robert Grosseteste (c. 1175-1253) and the Franciscan philosopher and *Doctor mirabilis* Roger Bacon (c. 1214-1292/4) who, with their contemporary Ramon Lull (c. 1235-1315), made genuine attempts to incorporate Arab-Islamic learning into a *Reformatio* in which, as Dr Ray Petry has said, 'The deepest and most pervasive action was held traceable to the most inward and sometimes the least perceptible *contemplatio*. *Theoria* and *praxis*, with overtones strange to our ears, were always conjoined in them' ('Essays in Divinity III' 1968, p. 96).

The pre-Reformation English mystics such as Richard Rolle of Hampole (ob. 1349) display many signs of traditional understanding. Rolle came under Franciscan influence while he was at Oxford and at the age of eighteen adopted the life of a wandering solitary, during which time he experienced moments of great spiritual joy. His lack of a firm background from which to operate led him to extremes of individualism only partially modified by his deep understanding of the early fathers, notably St Augustine and St Bernard.

A more substantial writer was the author of *The Cloud of Unknowing*, a theologian and probably a member of a religious order. The same author, whose name is unknown to us, was almost certainly the translator of an English version of Dionysius the Aregopagite's *Mystical Theology*, under the title *Dionise Hid Divinity*, a work which had a profound and prolonged influence on English religious thought. The third writer of this period was Walter Hilton (ob. 1396), an Augustinian Canon and head of the priory at Thugarton in Northamptonshire. His chief work is the *Scala Perfectionis*, an authentic account of the stages in the journey of the soul towards Perfection. Of these three writers the author of *The Cloud of Unknowing* has stood the test of time best and is widely read to this day. The reason for this may well be that his strong emphasis on the *via negativa* is most closely in touch with those teachings from the East which follow a similar path. The last of the mystics of this period was the unknown anchoress known as Dame Julian of Norwich (*c.* 1342-1414). A considerable cult has recently arisen centered on her and her home town of Norwich and copious, if often trivial, literature about her has flooded the market. The indigenous flowering of mysticism in Britain in the second half of the 14th century merged into a more diffused expression of spiritual longing based on Franciscan piety and the works of the Rhineland Mystics.

The 14th and 15th centuries were the ages of cathedral and church building and much work still remains to be done on the nature of the masonic fraternities in England and also the relation of the suppressed order of Templars (1312) and the evolution of a specifically Scottish masonic teaching.

Towards the end of the 15th century a fresh stream surfaced in Italy with the foundation by Marsilio Ficino of a Platonic Academy in Florence in about 1450. Ficino was taught by Eastern Orthodox teachers and translated Plato. He was visited by scholars from all over Europe, including John Colet, Dean of St Paul's, who was a great admirer of the works of the Pseudo-Dionysius. To sum up, we may quote the words of Dr Francis Yates on religious hermetism in the sixteenth century in England:

As compared with the intense preoccupation with religious hermetism in Europe . . . England was in a curious position of isolation . . . the adaptation of Catholic theology and philosophy to Neoplatonism and the *prisca theologia* made a beginning in England with Thomas More, John Colet, and their circle.

Colet was also greatly influenced by Pico de Mirandola and translated a biography of him into English. Pico was the first Christian Kabbalist and endeavoured to reconcile the two forms of esoteric teaching.

It is interesting to note that the modern secret cult with Gurdieffian connections known, amongst other names, as 'The School of Economic Science' has adopted Marsilio Ficino as a cultic hero. Needless to say, this perversion has nothing to do with any genuine teaching of tradition.

During the disturbed reigns of Elizabeth and Mary interest in the hermetic tradition was limited to private groups, such as that centred on Sir Philip Sidney, who had close connections with the Elizabethan Magus, John Dee (1527–1608) of whom Dr Yates wrote 'An isolated and lonely figure, the modern Magus collects the spiritual and also scientific treasures from those great ruins which towered in broken majesty over the Elizabethan scene'.

It cannot be too strongly emphasized that there is as yet no clear evidence of any sure filiation linking the various figures surveying the ruins caused by the Reformation and the rise of Protestanism in England, with an authentic traditional source. The Protestant Reformation, whether for good or ill, shattered the unity of Christendom which had been unsteadily preserved by the Catholic Church. Perhaps, looking back, we may conclude that this rupture was a necessary and inevitable stage in the current cycle's movement away from its primordial centre.

Dee is still a very enigmatic figure whose experiences in exile in Bohemia at the Court of the Emperor Rudolph and whose connections with esotericism there have still to be elucidated. Dee's successor in England was Robert Fludd (1774–1637), a great exponent of the notion of cosmic harmony, multiple levels of existence, and their mutual dependence. He belived truth to be universal and embraced a wide range of sources, both Christian and non-Christian, and in this was far ahead of his time.

A scholar in the Dee tradition was Elias Ashmole (1617–1692) the chief representative of the revived alchemical movement in England, whose vast legacy of papers in the Bodleian library has still to be examined in detail, especially with reference to his interest in, and connection with, the Rosicrucian Manifestos. Ashmole's chief work the *Theatrum Chemicum Britannicum* is a monument to English alchemists such as Norton and Ripley. This work was one of Sir Isaac Newton's chief sources of information on alchemy and Rosicrucians, in both of which he was deeply interested.

The belief that the Reformation had also a liberating and positive effect, as well as a negative and destructive one, is supported by the fact that the next figure of importance in England was a German Lutheran, the theosophist Jacob Boehme (1575–1624) known in England as Behmen. After his death, his works were circulated widely on the continent by his disciple J. G. Gichtel (1638–1710), resident in Amsterdam. By the middle of the seventeenth century they were circulating in manuscript in England and had attracted the notice of King Charles I, who sent an unemployed barrister named John Sparrow to the continent to collect Boehme's works and translate them into English, which he did. Sparrow subsequently became one of Boehme's earliest adherents and expositors in England. Gichtel founded various Behmenist groups in Amsterdam and was in contact with two Englishmen, Francis Lee (1661–1719) and Dr John Pordage (1607–1681), who were the two forces behind the foundation of The Philadelphian Society whose leading figure was the mystic and prophetess Jane Leade (1623–1724). All of the above three people wrote extensively, although Lee eventually returned to a more conventional religious path. The whole movement, ineffectual as it was, nevertheless represented a genuine attempt to restore certain beliefs which had been lost in the Reformation and Puritan revolutions.

A more interesting figure in The Age of Enlightenment was the poet and mystic William Blake (1757–1827), an admirer of Boehme whose works he read. His wide reading also included the translation by Sir Charles Wilkins (1749–1836) of the *Bhagavadgita* published in 1785. Wilkins, in company with other early members of the East India Company, notably Sir William Jones (1746–1794), was deeply interested in ancient Indian philosophy and religion, and both were notable Sanskrit scholars. But as the nineteenth century progressed, materialist considerations took over, and the nabobs of the East India Company were more interested in making their fortunes than in studying ancient philosophies.

One figure however stands out in the English Romantic revival as notably interesting and that is the poet, philosopher and theologian Samuel Taylor Coleridge (1772-1834). Coleridge was not only an ardent admirer of Boehme from his schooldays onward, but also the greatest interpreter in England of the German Romantic philosophers. His manuscript annotations to an edition of Boehme's works given to him by Thomas de Quincey have recently been published and would repay detailed study, as would many other of his manuscript writings.

The religious counterpart of the Romantic movement in literature was the revival of Catholic Christianity associated with Cardinal Newman (1801-1890) and known as the Oxford Movement. Patristic studies were revived and a sincere attempt made to restore to a debased Christianity some of its traditional teachings.

An important figure in the chain of students of Boehme was Mrs A.J. Penny, née Brown (1825-1893). She became interested in Boehme and L.C. de St Martin and with her husband Edward Burton Penny edited some of St Martin's correspondence and wrote many studies of Boehme's thought.

The rise of the Theosophical Movement renewed interest in Eastern philosophy and gave a focus to many small fringe Christian groups such as *The Association of St John the Evangelist* and *The Christo-Theosophical Society*, both founded by the Rev G.W. Allen, vicar of St James's, Bradford.

Concurrently with the rise of the Theosophical Society came the establishment of a host of pseudo-occult societies claiming filitation with earlier Rosicrucian and other reputable bodies. The most famous of these was The Hermetic Order of the Golden Dawn whose sorry history has been accurately chronicled by Ellic Howe in *The Magicians of the Golden Dawn*. In spite of its many dubious aspects the Order did attract at least two figures of importance, A.E. Waite (1857-1942) and W.B. Yeats (1861-1940). Waite's studies of Rosicrucianism and other aspects of Occult and Traditional lore are balanced and reasonably trustworthy. Yeats' knowledge of the Hermetic Tradition has been the subject of some recent studies which seem to indicate that his knowledge was more extensive and accurate than had hitherto been thought.

The inter-war years saw the publication of some of Guénon's works in English translated by the late Lord Northbourne and others (see Bibliography). In this period, also, the works of the Quaker Stephen Hobhouse on William Law (1680-1761) and his links with Boehme are worthy of note as exemplifying the value of the Quaker contribution to an authentic undogmatic spirituality.

We would also draw attention to the rise of a genuine interest in Vedanta and to the works of Radakrishnan on the *Bhagavad-gita* and Eastern philosophy. Guénon had a restricted but powerful influence which has grown since his death in 1951 and it is to be found in the works of Frithjof Schuon, Gai Eaton, Martin Lings, and others. Schuon was a long-time associate and student of Guénon but was eventually rejected by him and has developed his own special understanding, with his own devoted followers.

There are now in England and the USA authentic Muslim *tarigeh* offering initiation, and in a less dogmatic way the Ibn Arabi Society is working modestly to maintain a witness to true Islamic tradition. Buddhism in its various forms and Vedanta have their authentic expositors and many valuable texts have been translated.

Among writers on Buddhism one may mention D.T. Suzuki, Edward Conze, and Marco Pallis as being reliable guides.

The post-war scene is by and large too close and too confused to be susceptible to the necessary degree of objective assessment. A vast number of so-called Eastern *gurus* have risen and found followers. Societies, secret, semi-secret, and sensational, have arisen. White and black magical circles abound, most large towns have their witches' coven, and fringe religious groups come and go continuously.

The genuine seeker for authentic esoteric teaching is bewildered and needs to proceed with the utmost caution. The following very simple precautions may help to avoid disappointment or worse.

One: Beware of those who profess to reveal the secrets of any known occult organization; they have nothing worthwhile to offer.

Two: Beware of those who offer power by denying the seeker freedom of choice and the freedom to withdraw if they wish to, without threats of harassment.

Three: Beware of those organizations which obviously have plenty of money and buy expensive houses and give their leaders gold-plated Rolls Royces.

The number remaining, who are trustworthy will be very small indeed and you may well find the most accessible authentic teaching in certain members of the Christian churches.

Conclusion

The truly wise man is not
attached to any one
formulation of belief.
Ibn Arabi

In our search for truth each one of us will start from a different
point. Nobody's belief in God is identical with that of anyone else,
simply because our understanding depends so much on our
individual history. Nobody, even though he uses the same words
as others, professes the same faith. Our image of our God varies
according to the direction taken by our path in life. It is this sort
of metamorphosis of ideas which should be brought about by
the realization of metaphysics.

Our most orthodox beliefs remain implicit to such an extent
that we are unable to explain them to anyone else, even our closest
friend. In the same way the ineffable Principle remains esoteric,
supreme in the beyond, beyond all possible beyonds, the hidden
face of the unknowable.

But to achieve this transformation we are necessarily adherents
of one of the great historical traditions and we have to walk on
one of the world's spiritual paths. Differing circumstances have
meant that each one of these traditions has laid special emphasis on a different element or special virtue. India lays supreme
emphasis on sacrifice, Buddhism exalts charity, and Christianity
love. Judaism and Islam exalt the Principial Unity. Taoism and Zen
stress our need for sincerity and simplicity. But it is not our choice
of one or other of these characteristics which makes us choose
one or other of these traditions.

By birth, residence, or chance we are members of a particular nation and adherents to a particular religion which it seems natural for us to accept, for nothing can replace the path of our forebears to lead us back to the way of the Gods. When we have been prematurely attracted by some exotic form, our subconscious will protest and will urge us to stay in the old familiar path by thwarting our most carefully thought out intentions. Adopting a new path is a convenient excuse for avoiding a true conversion, which consists in inner change of direction (*metanoia*) from the human to the divine.

Our inherited path for purely practical reasons is best, since we are bound to it by psychic, intellectual, and emotional ties, and our spirituality consists in the synthesis and elevation of these ties. All spiritual symbolism possesses an 'aura' which is the result of its origins and is tinged with the colour of place, time, and language. Adaptation to a new and alien way is no easier than the conscious acceptance of and a clear-minded penetration into the deeper meaning of the old. It is better to accept our own national tradition, which we are free to go more deeply into if we can. For whatever we may do from the deepest recesses of our own hearts to the darkness of the Sublime, the path, as Plotinus has said, always leads from the alone to the Alone.

This rule, which is most applicable in stable and well-balanced epochs, admits of many exceptions in times such as ours when men and ideas are in such confusion. When a traditional rite, without being deprived of the efficacy of its rituals nevertheless no longer seems to provide acceptable means for self-realization, then it is legitimate for those who feel it is their destiny, to follow a different path. For from the point of view of the Hermetic tradition there is no question of conversion but only the acknowledgement of the one eternal truth in a more immediately accessible guise.

For the 'gift of tongues' is the supreme gift of the intellect. If it is accompanied by a sense of proportion and a discerning spirit, it enables us to lay hold on the truth in whatever form it is manifest. If this intelligence is absent we run into a mass of verbal quarrels which in reality do no more than reveal our differing capacities to think abstractly.

No master has ever revealed to anyone that secret spoken of in the Zohar and on which the world is based. But disciples with sufficient discernment can catch a glimpse of it through the transparent veil of secrecy which is the final alibi for our ignorance and the last disguise of Truth.

Bibliography

The following list of books is inevitably highly selective and represents one student's choice from among the enormous number of books on related subjects. For Part One the key works are those of René Guénon. For Part Two I have divided the works into those dealing with I) Oriental and II) Christian religions, in conformity with the author's division of his subject matter.

RW

Part One

ALLENDY, R., *Le Symbolisme des Nombres* (Paris, 1984).
  One of the most balanced and complete works in a field beset with amateurs.
FRANZ, M.-L. von, *Number and Time* (1974).
  Valuable for its non-mathematical approach.
GEORGEL, G., *Les Quatres Ages de l'humanité* (Milano, 1976).
——*Les Rhythmes dans l'Histoire* (Milano, 1981).
  The best writer on cosmic cycles, he received help from Guénon.
GUENON, René, *East and West* (1941).
——*The Crisis of the Modern World* (1942).
——*Introduction to the Study of the Hindu Doctrines* (1945).
——*Man and His Becoming According to the Vedanta* (1945).
——*The Reign of Quantity* (1953).
——*The Multiple States of Being* (New York, 1984).
SCHWALLER de LUBICZ, R.A., *Propos sur Esoterisme et Symbole* (Paris, 1977).
  An excellent work. An English edition is in preparation.
SCHUON, F., *Esoterism as Principle and as Way* (1981).
——*Gnosis: Divine Wisdom* (1959).

WATERFIELD, Robin, *René Guénon and the Future of the West* (1987).
The first work in English on Guénon's life and work, with a good bibliography.

Part Two

I. Oriental

I Ching or Book of Changes. The Richard Wilheim translation (1978).
The standard edition.
CONZE, E., *Buddhist Wisdom Books* (1970).
——ed. *Buddhist Texts through the Ages* (Oxford, 1954).
CRAGG, K., *The Call of the Minaret.*
The classic Christian-Muslim encounter.
DEUTSCH, E., *Advaita Vedanta* (Honolulu, 1980).
An excellent introduction.
ELIADE, M., *Yoga, Immortality, and Freedom* (1969).
Somewhat overstresses the historical objective approach. All Eliade's works are of value.
FEUERSTEIN, G., *The Philosophy of Classical Yoga* (New York, 1980).
KADOWAKI, J.K., *Zen and the Bible* (1987).
By a Japanese Jesuit. A very informed and sympathetic study.
LAO TZU, *Tao Te Ching.* The Richard Wilhelm Edition (1985).
Valuable scholarly edition with copious notes.
MASUNAGA, R., *A Primer of Soto Zen* (1984).
NASR, S.H., *Living Sufism* (1980).
PALLIS, M., *The Way and the Mountain.*
Full of valuable teaching, by a practising Western Buddhist.
——*Peaks and Lamas* (1939).
PANIKKAR, R., *The Vedic Experience: An Anthology of Vedas* (1979).
RULAND, V., *Eight Sacred Horizons: The Religious Imagination East and West* (1985).
Somewhat infected with Western scientific analytic attitudes but of value.
SCHAYA, L., *La Creation en Dieu à la lumiere du judaisme, du chris-tianisme, et de l'islam* (Paris, 1983).
A long and very valuable study.
SCHOLEM, G., *Major Trends in Jewish Mysticism* (1955).
An essential work.
SIRAT, C., *La Philosophie Juive au Moyen Age selon les testes MS et imprimés* (Paris, 1983).

VULLIAUD, P., *La Kabbale Juive* (s.l. Editions d'Aujourd'hui, 1976).
Two volumes. A standard work.
WATTS, A., *A Way of Zen* (New York, 1957).

II. Western

The Nag Hammadi Library, in English (Leiden, 1977).
Includes the Gospel of Thomas and all the other Gnostic Texts.
The Cloud of Unknowing (Oxford EETS, 1958).
ANDERSON, W., *Dante the Maker* (New York, 1982).
The best introduction to his work.
——With introductory Commentary and Translation by Ira Progoff.
(New York, 1961).
CUSANUS, Nicholas, *Of Learned Ignorance* (1954).
ECKHART, Meister, [Works] *by Franz Pfeiffer.* Translation by C. de
B. Evans (1947).
Two volumes. Best English edition.
FEDOTOV, G.P., *A Treasury of Russian Spirituality* (1952).
FRENCH, Peter J., *John Dee: the world of an Elizabethan Magus*
(1972).
GODWIN, Joscelyn, *Robert Fludd* (1979).
HILTON, W., *The Scale of Perfection,* ed. E. Underhill (1923).
HUTIN, Serge, *Les disciples anglais de Jacob Boehme* (Paris, 1960).
HURST, Desirée, *Hidden Riches: Traditional Symbolism from the
Renaissance to Blake* (1964).
HOWE, Ellic, *The Magicians of the Golden Dawn* (1972).
JOHNSTON, W., *The Mysticism of the Cloud of Unknowing* (1978).
Many comparisons with Zen teaching in which the author is
expert.
JULIAN OF NORWICH, *Revelations of Divine Love,* ed. G. Warrack
(1952).
KADLOUBOVSKY, E. and PALMER, G.E.H., trans., *Writings from
the Philokalia on Prayer of the Heart* (1951).
——*Early Fathers from the Philokalia . . . with some writings of St
Abba Dorotheus, St Isaac of Syria, and St Gregory Palamas* (1981).
KOYRE, A., *La Philosophie de Jacob Boehme* (Paris, 1929).
The best single work.
LECLERCQ, J., *The Love of Learning and the Desire for God* (1978).
Valuable for an understanding of the monastic tradition.
LOSSKY, V., *The Mystical Theology of the Eastern Church*
(1957).
NIGG, W., *Heimliche Weisheit: Mystisches Leben in der evangelischen
Christenheit* (Zurich u. Munich).

Excellent studies of Boehme, Angelus Silesius, Gichtel, Poiret et al.

PENNY, A.J., *Studies in Jacob Boehme* (New York, 1912).

PSEUDO-DIONYSIUS, *The Divine Names and Mystical Theology* (1920).

ROLLE, R. and HORSTMAN, C., *Richard Rolle and his Followers* (1895).

ROLLE, R., *Writings ascribed to Richard Rolle* (New York, 1927). Edited by H.E. Allen.

RUDOLPH, K., *Gnosis: The nature and history of an ancient religion* (1983).

SEDIR (pseud of I. Leloup), *Histoire et Doctrines des Rose-Croix* (Bihorel, 1932).
Of great value.

THUNE, N., 'Behmenists and Philadelphians' (Ph.D. Upsala, 1948).

UNDERHILL, E., *The Mystics of the Church* (1975).

WAITE, A.E., *Real History of the Rosicrucians* (New York, 1977).

WALKER, D.P., *Spiritual and Demonic Magic from Ficino to Campanella* (1958).

YATES, Frances A., *The Occult Philosophy in the Elizabethan Age* (1979).

——*The Rosicrucian Enlightenment* (1972).

——*Giordano Bruno and the Hermetic Tradition* (1964).